Celebrating Our Faith

Reconciliation
Teaching Guide

Principal Program Consultant
Dr. Jane Marie Osterholt, SP

BROWN-ROA
A Division of Harcourt Brace & Company

Nihil Obstat
Rev. Richard L. Schaefer

Imprimatur
✠ Most Rev. Jerome Hanus OSB
Archbishop of Dubuque
August 1, 1998
Feast of Saint Alphonsus Liguori
Patron of Confessors

The Ad Hoc Committee to Oversee the Use of the Catechism, National Conference of Catholic Bishops, has found this catechetical series to be in conformity with the *Catechism of the Catholic Church*.

The nihil obstat and imprimatur are official declarations that a book or pamphlet is free of doctrinal and moral error. No implication is contained herein that those who granted the nihil obstat and imprimatur agree with the contents, opinions, or statements expressed.

BROWN-ROA
A Division of Harcourt Brace & Company

Our Mission

The primary mission of BROWN-ROA is to provide the Catholic markets with the highest quality catechetical print and media resources. The content of these resources reflects the best insights of current theology, methodology, and pedagogical research. These resources are practical and easy to use, designed to meet expressed market needs, and written to reflect the teachings of the Catholic Church.

Photography Credits
Cover: Stained-glass windows at Zimmerman Chapel, United Theological Seminary, Dayton, Ohio. Photography by Andy Snow Photographics.
Gene Plaisted/The Crosiers: 11, 18, 63(c); **Digital Imaging Group:** 10(bl), 14, 15, 19, 23, 26, 34, 35, 38, 38, 42, 51, 51, 59, 62(c), 63(bl), 63(tl), 64(bl), 64(c); **FPG International:** Bill Losh: 30; Telegraph Colour Library: 6; **Jack Holtel:** 27; **PhotoEdit:** Tony Freeman: 22; David Young-Wolff: 46; **Andy Snow Photographics:** 10(c), 39, 43, 47, 50, 61, 62, 64(tl); **Tony Stone Images:** Stewart Cohen: 31; Peter Poulides: 7. Special thanks to the parish communities at St. Charles Borromeo, Kettering; St. Paul's, Oakwood; and Holy Angels, Dayton, for cooperation with photography.

Illustration Credits
Biblical Art: Chris Vallo/The Mazer Corporation: 8–9, 16–17, 24–25, 32–33, 40–41, 48–49; **Children's Art:** 12–13, 20–21, 28–29, 36–37, 44–45, 52–53 (prepared by Chelsea Arney, Lisol Arney, Kaley Bartosik, Hannah Berry, Noah Berry, Morgan Brickley, Brittany King, Cecily King, Jackie Malone, Katie Malone, Bob Ninneman, Claudia Ninneman, Erica Ninneman, Laura Grace Ninneman, Brittany Smith, Lauren Vallo, Ryan Vallo, and the art classes of Holy Angels School, Dayton)

Printed in the United States of America.
ISBN 0-15-950459-7

10 9 8 7 6 5 4 3 2

Celebrating Our Faith

Reconciliation
Teaching Guide

Introductory Material

Program Overview **T5**

Program Components **T6**

Scope and Sequence **T8**

Using the Teaching Guide **T10**

Lesson Plan Pages

My First Reconciliation **4**

A Blessing for Beginnings **5**

Chapter 1
We Belong 5a

Chapter 2
We Celebrate God's Love 13a

Chapter 3
We Hear Good News 21a

Chapter 4
We Look at Our Lives 29a

Chapter 5
We Ask Forgiveness 37a

Chapter 6
We Go Forth in Pardon and Peace 45a

Catholic Prayers **54**

Our Moral Guide **56**

An Examination of Conscience **59**

Celebrating the Sacrament of Reconciliation **60**

Illustrated Glossary **62**

Teaching Resources

Handouts and Activities **HA1**

First Reconciliation Family Retreat **R1**

Family Preparation Pages **F1**

Celebrating Other Sacraments **S1**

Celebrating Our Faith

Program Overview

Celebrating Our Faith offers a new approach to preparing children for the sacraments. Following the initiatory model of catechesis, *Celebrating Our Faith*

- begins with children's life experience.
- invites children to share our Christian story in Scripture.
- provides a "close-up" view and a lively explanation of the key liturgical moments of the sacramental celebrations.
- offers opportunities to reflect on, apply, and celebrate in prayer the chapter content.

While the sacramental preparation of children is less about the formal communication of doctrine than it is about welcoming children into the sacramental life of the community, *Celebrating Our Faith* materials have been developed in faithfulness to the *Catechism of the Catholic Church.*

Celebrating Our Faith materials involve families intimately in the preparation of children for the sacraments and recognize the primacy of the family. These are grace-filled opportunities to catechize adults as well as children. Program materials and activities also facilitate the involvement and support of the whole parish community.

Sacramental preparation materials are not intended to substitute for the ongoing religious education of children and young people. However, *Celebrating Our Faith* materials have been designed to complement BROWN-ROA's *Walking by Faith* basal religious education program as well as religious education materials from other publishers.

AGE ADAPTATIONS

Celebrating Our Faith: Eucharist and *Celebrating Our Faith: Reconciliation* are designed for use with children in grades 2–4.

- With children in primary grades, the catechist is encouraged to read the text aloud or to summarize it in his or her own words. Children six or seven years of age will need more help with the religious vocabulary than will older children. But remember that children do not have a mature understanding of difficult faith concepts. They will "grow into" the language of faith over time.
- When working with children eight, nine, ten, or older, you may wish to make additional resources, such as books and videos, available to supplement the text.

See the *Library Links* section of each chapter's planning pages in the Teaching Guide for suggested resources.
- Children in grades 3 and above are often preparing to celebrate Baptism and/or Confirmation as well as First Reconciliation and/or First Communion. For suggestions on preparing for these other sacraments, see *Celebrating Other Sacraments* in the Reconciliation Teaching Guide and *Preparing Children for Confirmation and First Communion* in the Eucharist Teaching Guide.

Program Components
Celebrating Our Faith
Reconciliation

Child's Book
- One colorful and engaging child's book for both school and parish
- Six 8-page content chapters based on the Rite of Penance
- Chapter structure flows from the catechetical process:
    We Are Invited—connects chapter theme to child's experience
    We Remember—retells a Scripture story related to the theme
    We Celebrate—explores the liturgical expression of the theme
    We Live Reconciliation—helps children apply the chapter content and celebrate it in prayer
- Content presented both verbally and visually
- *We Ask* feature puts doctrinal foundation from the *Catechism of the Catholic Church* into the form of commonly asked questions and answers for children and families to share
- Additional child's book resources include:
    Catholic Prayers—texts of common prayers for children
    Our Moral Guide—Beatitudes, commandments, precepts of the Church, works of mercy, plus an examination of conscience
    Celebrating the Sacrament of Reconciliation—review of the steps in the communal and individual celebrations of the Rite of Penance
    Illustrated Glossary—photographs and descriptions of the people, places, and objects associated with the Sacrament of Reconciliation

Note: The child's book is available in English or in a bilingual Spanish/English edition.

Teaching Guide
- One all-purpose Teaching Guide for school and parish
- Features full-color reduced child's book pages with a wraparound lesson plan
- Includes complete planning pages for each chapter session
- Back-of-the-book Teaching Resources include:
    Handouts and Activities—reproducible scripts, prayer services, and activities
    First Reconciliation Family Retreat—everything you need to plan, carry out, and evaluate a retreat for candidates and their families

Family Preparation Pages—reproducible lesson plans for use by adult family members preparing children for the sacraments at home or in neighborhood clusters
Celebrating Other Sacraments—notes on preparing children for the Sacraments of Initiation

Note: The Teaching Guide is available in English or Spanish. The Spanish version features reduced pages from the bilingual child's book.

Sharing Pages
- Designed to connect the catechetical experience with the home and family
- One Sharing Page per chapter
- Each Sharing Page contains:
    Family Note—summarizes the chapter content
    Living Reconciliation—suggestions for family activities to extend and enrich the catechetical experience
    Family Prayer—examples of family prayer
- The front of each Sharing Page features a colorful sacramental symbol tied to the chapter content

Note: The Sharing Pages are available in English, Spanish, Polish, or Tagalog.

My Reconciliation Book
- A 16-page two-color booklet containing the prayers and actions of the Rite of Penance (both communal and individual celebrations)
- Illustrated with line drawings of important liturgical moments for children to color
- Allows children to review the prayers and actions associated with the Rite of Penance
- A sturdy, colorful cover so children can keep the booklet to use in subsequent celebrations of the sacrament

Note: *My Reconciliation Book* is available in English or Spanish.

Celebrating Reconciliation with Children
Six 5-minute video segments for classroom or home use

Celebrating Reconciliation with Families
Two 40-minute video segments for meeting, retreat, or home use

Celebrating Our Faith Music
A collection of songs from GIA, distributed by BROWN-ROA, suitable for enhancing prayer and liturgy (available on CD or cassette)

Celebrating Our Faith
Eucharist

Child's Book
- One colorful and engaging child's book for both school and parish
- Eight 8-page content chapters based on the Order of the Mass
- Chapter structure flows from the catechetical process:

    We Are Invited—connects chapter theme to child's experience

    We Remember—retells a Scripture story related to the theme

    We Celebrate—explores the liturgical expression of the theme

    We Live the Eucharist—helps children apply the chapter content and celebrate it in prayer
- Content presented both verbally and visually
- *We Ask* feature puts doctrinal foundation from the *Catechism of the Catholic Church* into the form of commonly asked questions and answers for children and families to share
- Additional child's book resources include:

    Catholic Prayers—texts of common prayers for children

    The Life of Jesus—summary of key events in Christ's life

    Holy Communion—review of the Church's rules for receiving Holy Communion and the steps for receiving Communion under both forms

    Illustrated Glossary of the Mass—photographs and descriptions of the people, places, and objects associated with the Eucharistic liturgy

Note: The child's book is available in English or in a bilingual Spanish/English edition.

Teaching Guide
- One all-purpose Teaching Guide for school and parish
- Features full-color reduced child's book pages with a wraparound lesson plan
- Includes complete planning pages for each chapter session
- Back-of-the-book Teaching Resources include:

    Handouts and Activities—reproducible scripts, prayer services, and activities

    First Communion Family Retreat—everything you need to plan, carry out, and evaluate a retreat for candidates and their families

    Family Preparation Pages—reproducible lesson plans for use by parents and adult family members preparing children for the sacrament at home or in neighborhood clusters

    Preparing for Confirmation and First Communion—notes on completing children's initiation

Note: The Teaching Guide is available in English or Spanish. The Spanish version features reduced pages from the bilingual child's book.

Sharing Pages
- Designed to connect the catechetical experience with the home and family
- One Sharing Page per chapter
- Each Sharing Page contains:

    Family Note—summarizes the chapter content

    Living the Eucharist—suggestions for family activities to extend and enrich the catechetical experience

    Family Prayer—example of family prayer
- The front of each Sharing Page features a colorful sacramental symbol tied to the chapter content

Note: The Sharing Pages are available in English, Spanish, Polish, or Tagalog.

My Mass Book
- A 16-page two-color booklet containing the prayers and actions of the Mass
- Illustrated with line drawings of important liturgical moments for children to color
- Allows children to review the prayers and actions associated with the Order of the Mass
- A sturdy, colorful cover so children can keep the booklet to use at Mass after their First Communion

Note: *My Mass Book* is available in English or Spanish.

Celebrating Eucharist with Children
Eight 5-minute video segments for classroom or home use

Celebrating Eucharist with Families
Two 40-minute video segments for meeting, retreat, or home use

Celebrating Our Faith Music
A collection of songs from GIA, distributed by BROWN-ROA, suitable for enhancing prayer and liturgy (available on CD or cassette)

Scope and Sequence
Celebrating Our Faith
Reconciliation

	Key Theme	Scripture Story	Liturgical Connection	*We Ask* Catechism Reference
Chapter 1 We Belong				
	The Sacraments of Initiation make us part of the Church.	Paul shares the story of salvation (Acts 17:16–34)	Baptism, Confirmation, and Eucharist	Catechism, #1229–1233
Chapter 2 We Celebrate God's Love				
	The Sacrament of Reconciliation forgives sins committed after Baptism.	The Forgiving Father (Luke 15:11–32)	Two ways to celebrate Reconciliation	Catechism, #1855–1857
Chapter 3 We Hear Good News				
	God's word in the Scriptures reminds us of God's mercy and forgiveness.	The Lost Sheep (Luke 15:1–7)	Welcome and sharing of the Scriptures in the Rite of Penance	Catechism, #104, 1349
Chapter 4 We Look at Our Lives				
	We examine our conscience to prepare for confession.	The Ten Commandments, the Great Commandment (Luke 10:25–28)	The examination of conscience	Catechism, #1777, 1783
Chapter 5 We Ask Forgiveness				
	We confess our sins and accept a penance.	Zacchaeus (Luke 19:1–10)	Sacramental confession and the giving of a penance	Catechism, #1455–1456, 1467
Chapter 6 We Go Forth in Pardon and Peace				
	We pray an Act of Contrition and are absolved.	The Forgiven Woman (Luke 7:36–50)	The Act of Contrition, absolution, and dismissal in the Rite of Penance	Catechism, #1469

Scope and Sequence

Celebrating Our Faith
Eucharist

	Key Theme	Scripture Story	Liturgical Connection	*We Ask* Catechism Reference
Chapter 1 Belonging				
	The Sacraments of Initiation make us part of the Church.	Peter's Pentecost preaching *(Acts 2)*	Baptism and Confirmation	*Catechism, #1213*
Chapter 2 Invited to the Table				
	The Eucharist is a Sacrament of Initiation.	The Vine and the Branches *(John 15:1–17)*	First Communion	*Catechism, #1388*
Chapter 3 Gathering to Celebrate				
	We gather at Mass to celebrate the Eucharist.	The early Christians gather for Eucharist *(Acts 2:42–47)*	The Introductory Rites of the Mass	*Catechism, #2180–2182*
Chapter 4 Feasting on God's Word				
	We share God's word at Mass.	The Good Shepherd *(John 10:1–18)*	The Liturgy of the Word	*Catechism, #101–104*
Chapter 5 Offering Our Gifts				
	We offer our gifts to God at Mass.	Loaves and Fish *(John 6:5–13)*	The Presentation of Gifts	*Catechism, #1366–1368*
Chapter 6 Remembering and Giving Thanks				
	The Mass makes Jesus' sacrifice present.	The Last Supper *(Matthew 26:17–19, 26–28)*	The Eucharistic Prayer	*Catechism, #1333*
Chapter 7 Sharing the Bread of Life				
	We receive Jesus in Holy Communion.	The Bread of Life *(John 6:30–58)*	The Communion Rite at Mass	*Catechism, #1384–1389*
Chapter 8 Going Forth to Love and Serve				
	We have a mission to share God's love with others.	The Journey to Emmaus *(Luke 24:13–35)*	The Concluding Rite of the Mass	*Catechism, #1402–1405*

Using the Teaching Guide

This Teaching Guide has been developed to assist you in your ministry of preparing children to celebrate the sacraments. Whatever your level of catechetical experience, you will find this Teaching Guide to be your greatest ally in carrying out your ministry. But no Teaching Guide or child's book, no matter how comprehensive, can take the place of the personal witness of the catechist. You—with your experience, your faith, your commitment—are the best gift you bring to sacramental preparation.

Sacramental preparation is a mutual journey, a common pilgrimage undertaken together by children, catechists, families, and the parish community. On that journey you are encouraged to adapt the Teaching Guide strategies and suggestions to suit the needs of your particular catechetical community.

To assist family members who will be preparing their children for the sacraments at home, see the Family Preparation Pages (pages F1–F13). These pages feature reproducible lesson plans for home or neighborhood-cluster catechesis.

Preparing to Teach

Preceding each chapter in this Teaching Guide are two planning pages. These pages help you plan your lesson, organize materials, prepare yourself spiritually, and locate any additional resources you may need.

Before you teach each chapter:
- take time to review the planning pages
- read through the chapter lesson plan pages
- make notes on the steps you will follow and the optional activities you will carry out
- gather any necessary materials
- preview additional resources

Here is what you will find on the planning pages for each chapter.

Planning Chart

The planning chart provides a simple, easy-to-follow outline of the chapter. Each chapter is built around one 4-part session, corresponding to the *We Are Invited, We Remember, We Celebrate,* and *We Live* pages of the child's book. A section of the chart entitled *Pacing Guide* provides suggestions for allocating session time, with space for you to write in your own allocations. The planning chart also lists objectives for each part of the chapter and indicates any necessary materials or additional program resources.

Catechetical Background

This section of the planning pages provides a brief reflection on the doctrinal foundation of the chapter, linked to the Catechism reference in the *We Ask* feature in the child's book. You are encouraged to read the particular passages from the *Catechism of the Catholic Church* to add to your own understanding.

One-Minute Retreat

This feature gives you a way to prepare yourself spiritually to teach the chapter. A thought-provoking quotation focuses on the chapter theme. Reflection questions help you look at the chapter theme as it is lived out in your own experience. Finally, a brief prayer invites God to be present with you as you teach.

Library Links

This section of the planning pages offers annotated suggestions for additional resources tied to the chapter theme, including:

Books for Children These may be read to the children or suggested for outside reading. They are available in libraries or through publishers' catalogs.

Books for Adults These resources are intended for catechists and adult family members. They are available in libraries or through publishers' catalogs. **Note:** *Catholic Update,* a single-topic newsletter published by St. Anthony Messenger Press, offers many useful back issues on sacramental topics. These may be ordered at bulk rates from the publisher.

Multimedia for Children This section lists videos and music available from catalogs or through diocesan or parish media libraries. Resources for children may be shared in class or loaned to families for sharing at home.

Multimedia for Adults This section lists videos, audiotapes, and software available from catalogs or through diocesan or parish media libraries. Resources for adults are intended to enhance the understanding of catechists and adult family members.

Teaching a Chapter

Lesson Plan

The lesson plan pages of this Teaching Guide take you through the chapter in a simple, easy-to-follow process. Each lesson plan page consists of a full-color reduced version of the child's book page surrounded by a wraparound lesson plan. Next to the child's book page you will find the core lesson plan. These are the steps you will follow to communicate the chapter content.

Below the child's book page, across the bottom of the Teaching Guide page, you will find the Resource Center, which contains background information, links, tips, and optional enrichment activity suggestions.

The Core Lesson Plan

Each chapter is designed to be taught in one session. The chapter lesson plan is divided into three simple steps:

1. **Open**—strategies for introducing the chapter content
2. **Build**—strategies for developing the chapter content
3. **Close**—strategies for applying chapter content and ending the session with prayer

Here are some of the features of the core lesson plan column:

Gathering Suggestions for inviting the children into the session and connecting the chapter content with their everyday lives

Prayer Suggestions for praying the opening prayer and celebrating the closing prayer of the session

Working with the Text Teaching directions for exploring the words on the page. These simple steps include suggestions for reading aloud, working with vocabulary, and directing discussion

Working with the Pictures Teaching directions for exploring the photographs and illustrations on the page. Much of the important content of *Celebrating Our Faith* is communicated visually, and these steps will help you guide the children's understanding of what they see

Working with the Page Suggestions for carrying out in-text activities and prayer celebrations

We Ask Suggestions for working with this text feature, which asks and answers a common question related to the theme of the chapter, providing a background reference to the *Catechism of the Catholic Church*

Living Reconciliation at Home Suggestions for follow-up activities to be done with the family

Living Reconciliation in the Parish Suggestions for follow-up activities related to the liturgical community, including using *My Reconciliation Book*

Getting Ready for First Reconciliation Discussion questions geared toward helping children integrate chapter content into their personal preparation for the sacrament

The Resource Center

This section contains background features and optional activities to extend and enrich the core lesson. These features include:

Background (including Art, Scripture, Catechetical) Provides key information at point of use, to deepen your own and the children's understanding

The Language of Faith Introduces and develops the children's understanding of key religious vocabulary, with definitions rooted in the *Catechism of the Catholic Church*

Multicultural Link Offers information and optional activities for exploring the Church's global diversity

Link to the Family, Link to the Faith Community, Link to Liturgy Provide suggestions for linking the class to the home, the parish, and the liturgical life of the community

Meeting Individual Needs Offers strategies for adapting teaching situations to the various learning styles of the children

Teaching Tip Provides suggestions for classroom management, clarifying content, handling sensitive topics, and answering questions

Space for your own notes is provided at the beginning and end of the chapter.

My First Reconciliation

When you first distribute the children's books (at the first class session or at a preliminary family meeting or retreat), help the children fill out this page. Tell the children that by signing the page, they are asking the whole parish community to help them prepare for their First Reconciliation. Sign your name in the box in each child's book, and ask the children to have their family members, godparents, prayer partners, and classmates sign as well.

My First Reconciliation

**I will celebrate
the Sacrament of Reconciliation
for the first time
on**

_____
(date)

at

_____
(name of church)

**I ask my family, my godparents,
my teacher, my classmates, my friends,
and everyone in my parish community
to help me prepare for this celebration.**

_____
(signed)

**Here are the signatures of people who are helping
me prepare for my First Reconciliation.**

Resource Center

Link to the Faith Community

Work with parish ministers and interested parishioners to match each child with a parish prayer partner. Prayer partners may be older children, families, young adults, or elderly parishioners. Prayer partners agree to pray for the children they sponsor throughout the course of the children's sacramental preparation. Throughout this Teaching Guide you will find suggestions for activities children can share with their prayer partners. Children should not be partnered with adults without family approval and should be supervised when meeting with adult prayer partners.

A Blessing for Beginnings

"The Lord is merciful! He is kind and patient, and his love never fails."

—Psalm 103:8

Leader: Today we gather to begin your journey
toward First Reconciliation.
We are ready to learn from one another
and from our Church community.
And so we pray:
God our Father, show us your mercy and love.
Jesus, Son of God, deliver us from the power of sin.
Holy Spirit, help us grow in charity, justice,
and peace.

Reader: Listen to God's message to us:
(Read Ephesians 2:4–10.)
The word of the Lord.

All: **Thanks be to God.**

Leader: We ask God's blessing on our journey together.

All: **Holy Trinity, live in our hearts.
Teach us to love and forgive.
Help us turn to you in true sorrow for sin,
and trust in your never-ending mercy.
We pray in the words that Jesus taught us.**
(Pray the Lord's Prayer.)

Leader: May the Lord be with us, now and always.

All: **Amen!**

A Blessing for Beginnings : 5

A Blessing for Beginnings

Use this brief prayer service to begin your sacramental preparation. You may incorporate this service into your first session or schedule it as part of a family meeting before sessions begin. If possible, celebrate the service in the parish church. Invite the children's family members, godparents, and other interested parishioners to join you for the celebration.

- To prepare for the prayer service, choose a reader (a child or family member), and provide him or her with a Bible opened to **Ephesians 2:4–10**. Point out the part of the prayer service in which the reading occurs.

- Gather the children and any other participants. You may wish to play some instrumental music or sing one of the songs the children will be learning for First Reconciliation.

- Take the part of *Leader*. Invite the children and others present to follow along and respond together at the parts marked *All*.

- You may wish to include a gesture of blessing (traditionally, laying hands on the top of a person's head or signing him or her with a cross) to accompany the final blessing. If family members attend the prayer service, they may join you in blessing their children.

Teaching Tip

Celebrating this prayer service You may wish to incorporate this prayer service into a First Reconciliation family retreat (see page R1). If you are preparing the children to celebrate other sacraments, see page S1.

WE BELONG

Key Content Summary

We belong to the Catholic Church. We become members of the Catholic Church through the Sacraments of Initiation—Baptism, Confirmation, and Eucharist.

Planning the Chapter

Open	Pacing Guide *Suggested time/Your time*	Content	Objectives	Materials
	10–20 min./ ____ min.	We Are Invited, pp. 6–7	• Recognize the importance of belonging to a community and to the Church.	• music for prayer (optional)

Build				
	35–45 min./ ____ min.	We Remember, pp. 8–9	• Recall the saving events of the Paschal mystery—Jesus' life, death, and resurrection.	• world map or globe
		We Celebrate, pp. 10–11	• Identify the Sacraments of Initiation as the way we become members of the Catholic Church. • Describe the signs and words of the Sacraments of Baptism, Confirmation, and Eucharist.	

Close				
	15 min./ ____ min.	We Live Reconciliation, pp. 12–13	• Celebrate our belonging to the Church.	• writing or drawing materials • Chapter 1 *Sharing Page* • music for prayer (optional) • writing materials, chart paper (optional)

Catechism Background

Doctrinal Foundation The Sacraments of Initiation—Baptism, Confirmation, and Eucharist—

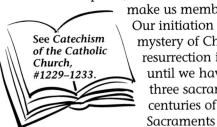

See *Catechism of the Catholic Church,* #1229–1233.

make us members of the Church. Our initiation into the Paschal mystery of Christ's death and resurrection is not complete until we have celebrated all three sacraments. In the early centuries of the Church, the Sacraments of Initiation were celebrated at the same time, as they are today in the Rite of Christian Initiation of Adults and in some Eastern and Latin Rite communities. In the experience of most Latin Rite Catholics, Confirmation has become separated from Baptism and often occurs years after First Communion. But whenever the Sacraments of Initiation are celebrated, they form a unity that moves from the new birth of Baptism, through the anointing by the Holy Spirit in Confirmation, to the sharing in Christ's Body and Blood at the table of the Eucharist. "God's Spirit baptized each of us and made us part of the body of Christ" *(1 Corinthians 12:13)*.

One-Minute Retreat

Read

"Christianity is more than a doctrine. It is Christ himself, living in those whom he has united to himself in one Mystical Body."

—*Thomas Merton*

Reflect

What does being a Christian mean to me?

How do I show that I am a member of the Body of Christ?

Pray

Jesus,
you have made me part of your own Body
in water and Spirit
and in the sacred Bread and Wine of the Eucharist.
Help me guide the children
to a fuller understanding of their Christian life
and their mission to share your love.
Amen.

Library Links

Books for Children

The Best Day Ever: The Story of Jesus, by Marilyn Lashbrook (Liguori).
Jesus' saving life, death, and resurrection recounted for children.

God Speaks to Us in Feeding Stories, by Gail Ramshaw (Liturgical Press).
Scripture stories with meal themes help children explore the connection between God's word and the Eucharist.

God Speaks to Us in Water Stories, by Mary Ann Getty-Sullivan (Liturgical Press).
Scripture stories with water themes help children explore the symbols of Baptism.

Books for Adults

A Child's Journey: The Christian Initiation of Children, by Rita Burns Senseman (St. Anthony Messenger Press).
A look at celebrating the Sacraments of Initiation with children of catechetical age.

"What Catholics Believe: A Popular Overview of Catholic Teaching," by Leonard Foley OFM (*Catholic Update*; St. Anthony Messenger Press).
While You Were Gone: A Handbook for Returning Catholics and Those Thinking About It, by Fr. William Bausch (Sheed & Ward).

Multimedia for Children

Celebrating Reconciliation with Children (6-part video series) (produced by Salt River Production Group; BROWN-ROA).
Segment 1: We Belong is designed for use with this chapter.

Celebrating Our Faith (CD) (produced by GIA; BROWN-ROA).
One or more songs from this collection may be used to enhance classroom prayer and liturgy.

The Sacraments for Children (video) (Liguori).
The seven sacraments and their relationship to one another.

Multimedia for Adults

What Makes Us Catholic? Discovering Our Catholic Identity (video) (Franciscan Communications/ St. Anthony Messenger Press).
The beliefs and customs Catholics share.

WE ARE INVITED

1. Open

Gathering Welcome the children to class, and tell them that you are looking forward to spending important times with them. Explain that they will learn more about God's great love for them and how the Church celebrates God's gift of forgiveness.

Prayer Pray the opening prayer aloud, inviting the children to repeat each line of the prayer after you. See *Music for Prayer* for suggested songs to accompany the opening prayer.

Working with the Pictures

Draw attention to the photograph on page 6.
How do you think these children belong to each other?
(Possible answers: They are friends; they are classmates; they belong to the same sports team or club.)

Working with the Text

Read aloud the text. Write the word *community* on the board. Use *The Language of Faith* to clarify the meaning of the word *community*.
What are some communities you belong to? (Possible answers: my family, my group of friends, my class, my sports team.)

WE BELONG

Dear God—Father, Son, and Holy Spirit— you have called us to be Christian. Help us always remain close to you. Amen!

Where do you belong?
  The people you share important times with and feel at home with are your **community**. Everyone needs to be part of a community. You weren't made to live alone in the world.

6 : We Are Invited

Resource Center

The Language of Faith

A **community** is a group of people who share time and space and who have common beliefs and activities. A Christian community is a special community because it shares a common belief in the Trinity and the Church. The Catholic community celebrates together the Mass and the sacraments.

Music for Prayer

Consider teaching the children a song for First Reconciliation based on the theme of community. Sing the song before or after the opening prayer. Other suggestions for music to enhance this prayer are "We Remember," "You Have Put on Christ," or "Sing Out Gladly" from the *Celebrating Our Faith* CD.

Teaching Tip

Handling sensitive topics Keep in mind that some children in your class may not feel as if they belong to any groups or communities or may simply be uncomfortable in a group situation. Assure the children that they belong to this class community. Express your gratitude and respect for each child.

Your family is a community. So is your group of friends. You belong to another important community, too. You belong to the **Catholic** Church.

Your Catholic community comes together to worship God at Mass. You celebrate the **sacraments** together. With other Catholic children you learn about God.

You may not know it, but your Catholic community is much bigger than the people you see at church on Sunday. The Church is a family as big as the whole world.

We Are Invited : 7

WE ARE INVITED
Open *Continued*

Working with the Text

• Write the words *Catholic Church* on the board. Underline *Catholic*.

• Read aloud the text. Then write the word *sacraments* on the board under *Catholic Church*.
  How does the Catholic community worship God together?
  (by celebrating Mass)
  What else does the Catholic community celebrate together?
  (the sacraments)

• Emphasize that the Catholic community can be found in every country of the world.

Working with the Pictures

Ask the children to look at the photograph on this page.
  What kind of a community do you see in this picture?
  (a church community)
  What are they doing together?
  (praying the Lord's Prayer at Mass)
  How do you know that they are a community?
  (Possible answers: They are sharing an important time together; they are all holding hands; they are all worshiping God together.)

The Language of Faith

• The **Catholic** Church is a Church that is open to all people. The word *catholic* means "universal" or "everywhere." The Catholic Church invites people of every race, country, and culture to be members and to worship God through the liturgy and the sacraments.

• The **sacraments** are celebrations, signs, and sources of God's grace. In the sacraments Jesus joins with the community in special words and actions. The Catholic Church celebrates seven sacraments.

Notes

_____

_____

_____

_____

_____

_____

Working with the Pictures

- Invite the children to study the illustration on page 8. Invite volunteers to describe what they see.
- Invite volunteers to speculate on what the story might be about.

Working with the Text

- Invite the children to find comfortable positions for sharing the Scripture story.
- Explain to them that this is a story about Saint Paul, a man who didn't know Jesus personally but who came to be one of Jesus' best friends and apostles.
- Tell the children that this story takes place in a country called Greece, in its famous city of Athens. Show the children on a map or globe where Greece is located.
- Read aloud or retell the story on page 8 in your own words.
  Why did Saint Paul travel to Greece? (to tell people about Jesus)
  Whom did the people of Greece worship? (many gods)

We Are God's Children

Saint Paul traveled to Greece to tell people about Jesus. In the city of Athens, Paul stood up in the marketplace.

"People of Athens!" Paul said. "I see that you worship many gods. Well, today I am going to tell you about the one true God so that you can come to know him."

8 : We Remember

Resource Center

Scripture Background

Paul's missionary journey to Athens, Greece, the cultural center of the known world, happened late in his missionary life and almost by accident. After having been thrown out of Berea, a city in Macedonia, Paul was waiting in Athens for his missionary companions to arrive and join him for a pilgrimage to Corinth, another important Greek city. Once in Athens, Paul met up with people who were already religious but who did not worship the one, true God. Paul tried to explain that the images or idols they worshiped did not contain any powers at all. Instead, all power rested with God the Father, who raised up Jesus, his only Son, bringing redemption to all humankind.

The Acts of the Apostles tell us that some people listened to Paul's teachings and became Christians, some ridiculed him, and some invited him to return to their city at a later date to tell them more about this one, true God.

Art Background

The illustration on page 8 depicts Paul's zealous preaching to the people of Athens. The marketplace was a very large area that was almost entirely surrounded by colonnades, some of which can be seen in the background of this illustration. It was common practice to gather in the marketplace to listen to great teachers, religious leaders, and philosophers.

Paul pointed to the blue sky. "God made all things. He made the sun and the moon and the stars. He gives life and breath to every person."

People began to listen closely. They wanted to know more.

"God made us all to be one family," Paul continued. "We are God's children, and he wants each of us to turn to him with love."

"How do you know these things?" someone asked.

Paul smiled. "God the Father sent his own Son, Jesus, to tell us all," he said. "Until now many people didn't know how much God loved them, so they turned away from him and sinned. But now everyone knows how strong God's love is. God the Father even raised Jesus from death!"

Some people laughed at Paul. But others believed him. They turned to God and became followers of Jesus.

—based on Acts 17:16–34

Build *Continued*
Working with the Text

- Continue reading or retelling the Scripture story.
  To whom did Paul tell the people we belong? (God and one another)
  How did Paul know this? (because God sent Jesus to tell us)
  How did people react to what Paul was telling them about the one, true God? (Some people laughed; others believed him and became followers of Jesus.)

- Point out to the children that Paul believed strongly in God the Father and in Jesus, God's Son.
  Why do you think Paul wanted others to believe as he did? (Paul was convinced that God loved him and all people deeply, and he wanted to share the good news of God's love with others.)

Working with the Pictures

Draw attention to the illustration of Jesus at the top of this page. Help the children recognize this as an illustration of Jesus risen from the dead. Invite volunteers to describe what else they see in the picture.
How does this picture show God's love for us? (Jesus was raised from the dead to save us from the power of sin and everlasting death when we turned away from God; the Earth is a symbol for the whole world that was created for us out of love.)

Art Background

The Scripture art at the top of this page depicts the risen Jesus holding a cross in his hand, a sign of his victory over sin and death. Earth, shown behind him, symbolizes the whole world created and sustained by God's love. The illustration sums up Paul's message to the people of Athens that God, out of deep love created everything good, including each of us. God the Father then sent his own Son, Jesus, to show us the depth of his love.

Teaching Tip

Clarifying concepts The children may ask why the people in this Scripture story worshiped many gods. Explain that most people in the days of Jesus and Paul did not understand as much about the world and how it came into being as we do today. It was common practice in those days to believe that different gods controlled different things in creation. For instance, many people believed that the sun-god controlled the sun and that another god was responsible for taking care of the animals. A God who created all and loved everyone and everything he created was a brand new idea for them. Yet Paul respected their beliefs and never made fun of them or ridiculed them.

Working with the Text

- Write the words *Baptism* and *initiation* on the board. Invite volunteers to describe what these words mean.

- Read aloud the text on this page. Point out that Baptism is the first sacrament we celebrate because it makes us members of the Church and gives us a share in God's life.

- Use *The Language of Faith* to deepen the children's understanding of the bold-faced words.

Working with the Pictures

- Direct attention to the large picture at the bottom of this page. **What do you see happening in the picture?** (A priest is baptizing the boy with water.)

- Tell the children that the priest uses these words when he baptizes: "I baptize you in the name of the Father, and of the Son, and of the Holy Spirit."

- Tell the children that the smaller picture on the page shows the Sacrament of Confirmation. Confirmation is another Sacrament of Initiation. In the picture the bishop is holding his hands over the head of the young girl in an ancient gesture called "the laying on of hands," through which the person is sealed with the gift of the Holy Spirit.

Sacraments of Initiation

Like the people who listened to Saint Paul, we became members of the Church by being baptized. In the Sacrament of **Baptism**, we become part of the Body of Christ.

But there is more to becoming a member of the Catholic community than being baptized. Baptism is the first of three Sacraments of Initiation. The word **initiation** means "becoming a member."

10 : We Celebrate

Resource Center

The Language of Faith

- The Sacrament of **Baptism** is always the first Sacrament of Initiation to be celebrated. Through this sacrament new members share in the Paschal mystery of our faith—the suffering, dying, and rising of Jesus and his ascension into glory. The word *baptism* means "bath." Water is one of the signs of Baptism. We are washed free of original sin and all personal sin.

- **Initiation** is the term used by the Church to describe the process by which those who wish to join the Church become members. To be initiated means "to be brought into the community." The

Church has three Sacraments of Initiation, each one bringing the person into fuller membership.

Link to Liturgy

At special times throughout the liturgical year, such as during the Easter Season, the Introductory Rites of the Mass sometimes include the renewal of baptismal vows and the sprinkling with holy water as a reminder of our Baptism. This rite takes the place of the Penitential Rite and acts as a reminder of what we believe as baptized Christians and how those beliefs call us to live our lives.

Confirmation is the second Sacrament of Initiation. In Confirmation we receive the Holy Spirit in a special way. We are joined even more closely to the Church community.

The third Sacrament of Initiation is the **Eucharist**. Of course, we celebrate the Eucharist every Sunday by taking part in the Mass. But when we receive Jesus in Holy Communion for the first time, we complete our initiation. First Communion makes us fully members of the Church because it joins us completely with Jesus and with one another.

We Ask

Why aren't the three Sacraments of Initiation always celebrated at the same time?

Early Christians were baptized, confirmed, and received into Eucharistic communion all at once. The same is true today for many adults and children of school age and for infants in the Eastern Rites of the Church. In the Latin Rite, Catholics baptized as infants usually receive First Communion around the age of seven and may celebrate Confirmation at that time or some time later.
(Catechism, #1229–1233)

We Celebrate : 11

WE CELEBRATE
Build *Continued*
Working with the Text

- Read aloud or summarize the text on this page.
- Use *The Language of Faith* to clarify the meanings of the bold-faced words.
- Help the children reflect on what they have learned by taking a few minutes to discuss the text. **What is the second Sacrament of Initiation?** (Confirmation) **Whom do we receive in a special way at Confirmation?** (the Holy Spirit) **Which Sacrament of Initiation can we receive again and again?** (Eucharist)

We Ask Invite a volunteer to read the question aloud. Then read the answer to the children, pausing to ensure that they understand each sentence. Explain the order in which the Sacraments of Initiation are usually celebrated in your parish or diocese. Remind the children to share this question and answer with their family members and prayer partners.

The Language of Faith

- The Sacrament of **Confirmation** is the sacrament that seals us with the Holy Spirit and completes Baptism. Once we are sealed with and confirmed in the Holy Spirit, we are strengthened to witness to the risen Jesus and to participate more fully in the life and mission of the Church.

- The Sacrament of the **Eucharist** is a sacrament that we are invited to celebrate often throughout our lives. Each time we receive Jesus in the Eucharist, we are united more deeply to him and to one another. The Eucharist is Jesus' Real Presence with his people.

Catechetical Background

Children of this age cannot be expected to understand fully the importance or significance of the Sacraments of Initiation, either as individual sacramental experiences or as a unit. Providing the children with the basis for developing an understanding of the Church's process of initiation is enough for now. As the children grow and continue into adulthood, they will also grow in their understanding of the Paschal mystery, into which all Catholics are baptized, confirmed, and brought to the Lord's table.

3. Close

Working with the Page

- Read the directions aloud. Be sure the children understand that they can draw or glue a picture of their Baptism in the space at the bottom of the certificate on this page.
- Assign the activity as a take-home project, since it calls for information that the children will need a family member's help to obtain.
- Make time during a later class for the children to share their work.

Living Reconciliation at Home

Suggest these follow-up activities.

- With your family, renew your baptismal vows by praying together the Apostles' Creed or the Nicene Creed. Then make the Sign of the Cross with holy water.
- Make a Sacraments Family Tree. For each family member, list the sacraments he or she has celebrated and the dates (or years) when they were celebrated.

Living Reconciliation in the Parish

Have the children complete these activities in class or at home with family members or prayer partners.

- Practice making the Sign of the Cross slowly and reverently.
- Look for ways in which your parish community uses the cross as a symbol—in church art, as jewelry, or on bumper stickers.

Getting Ready for First Reconciliation

Have the children work in small groups to discuss this question.

You will soon celebrate the Sacrament of Reconciliation for the first time. How will the Sacraments of Initiation help you live a life of forgiveness and loving service to others?

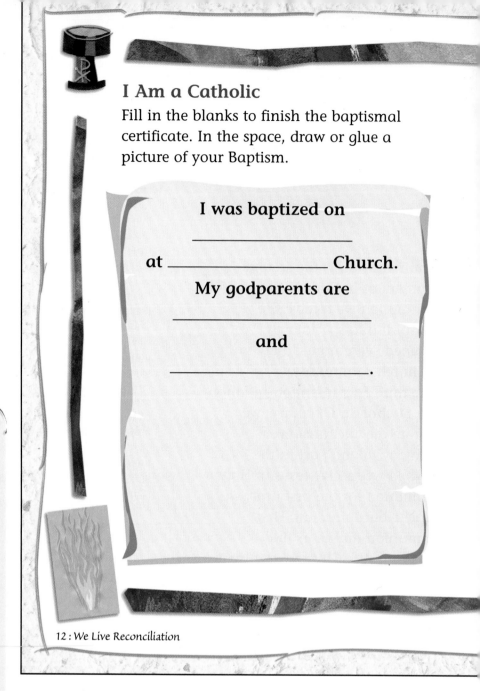

I Am a Catholic

Fill in the blanks to finish the baptismal certificate. In the space, draw or glue a picture of your Baptism.

I was baptized on

_____

at _____ Church.

My godparents are

_____

and

_____.

12 : We Live Reconciliation

Resource Center

Link to the Family

Distribute the Chapter 1 *Sharing Page* to be taken home. Encourage the children to take their books home to share with family members.

Children of One Family

We thank God for making us members of one family through the Sacraments of Initiation.

God, our loving Father,
because you love us,
you sent Jesus, your Son,
to bring us to you
and to gather us around him
as the children of one family.

Hosanna in the highest!

Jesus came to show us
how we could love you, Father,
by loving one another.
He came to take away sin and hate,
which keeps us from being friends,
and which makes us all unhappy.

Hosanna in the highest!

He promised to send the Holy Spirit,
to be with us always
so that we can live as your children.

Hosanna in the highest!

—*based on Eucharistic Prayer II for Children*

We Live Reconciliation : 13

Working with the Page

- Spend a few moments looking back through this chapter with the children. Ask volunteers to comment on their favorite part of the lesson or their favorite pictures.

- Direct the children's attention to the symbols that make up the page border. Invite volunteers to explain the connection between the symbols and the chapter theme. (The baptismal fonts and flames of the Holy Spirit are signs of the Sacraments of Initiation.)

- Have the children bring their books to the classroom prayer space or the church. Gather around a table or the baptismal font. If possible, have the children's families and their prayer partners join you for the prayer.

Prayer Teach the children the response to the prayer on this page: "Hosanna in the highest!" **Where else have you heard this prayer prayed?** (at Mass) Tell the children that this is also the prayer of praise people shouted as Jesus entered Jerusalem before he died. Lead the children in the prayer, beginning and ending with the Sign of the Cross. See *Music for Prayer* for suggested songs to accompany this closing prayer.

Music for Prayer

To enhance the prayer celebration, you may wish to have the children sing a musical setting of the "Holy, Holy, Holy Lord" used in your parish. Or you may wish to choose a song from the *Celebrating Our Faith* CD.

Enrichment

Write a class epistle Tell the children that another name for the letters Paul and other disciples of Jesus wrote to the early Christian communities is *epistles*. Help the class write an epistle of its own, telling the good news of the one, true God to another class of children in your parish's religious education program.

Notes

_____

_____

_____

_____

_____

_____

WE CELEBRATE GOD'S LOVE

Key Content Summary

Baptism forgives original sin and all personal sin. But because of free will, we can choose to sin. The Sacrament of Reconciliation celebrates God's continuing mercy and forgiveness.

Planning the Chapter

Open	Pacing Guide *Suggested time/Your time*	Content	Objectives	Materials
	10–20 min./ _____ min.	**We Are Invited**, pp. 14–15	• Recognize that we sin and need to ask forgiveness.	• music for prayer (optional)

Build				
	35–45 min./ _____ min.	**We Remember**, pp. 16–17	• Recall one of Jesus' parables about God's mercy and forgiveness.	• copies of script on pages HA3–HA4, simple costumes and props (optional)
		We Celebrate, pp. 18–19	• Identify the Sacrament of Reconciliation as our celebration of the forgiveness of sin.	
			• Describe two ways to celebrate the Sacrament of Reconciliation.	

Close				
	15 min./ _____ min.	**We Live Reconciliation**, pp. 20–21	• Celebrate God's love and mercy in our lives.	• writing or drawing materials • *My Reconciliation Book* • Chapter 2 *Sharing Page* • music for prayer (optional)

Catechism Background

Doctrinal Foundation   Consciousness of sin is the fundamental impulse of contrition and reconciliation. Like the prodigal son, we "come to ourselves" and recognize how far we have come from our Father's house. Mortal and venial sin differ in degree of seriousness, but all personal sin has the same root—turning away from God's loving will for us, deciding in our pride that we know best. The Sacrament of Reconciliation is both a reminder and a celebration of the wonderful truth Jesus shared in the parable: when we acknowledge our sin and ask forgiveness, God meets us more than halfway. "The Lord is merciful! He is kind and patient, and his love never fails" *(Psalm 103:8).*

See Catechism of the Catholic Church, #1855–1857.

One-Minute Retreat

Read

"Reconciliation sounds a large and theological term, but it simply means coming to ourselves and arising and going to our Father."

—*John Oman*

Reflect

When have I experienced true reconciliation in my life?

Who are the people who show me God's forgiving love?

Pray

Forgiving Father,
even when I wander away from your love,
you are there to meet me on the road home.
Keep me always open to your forgiveness and mercy,
and help me show the children
the way home to your constant love.
Amen.

Library Links

Books for Children
The Story of the Lost Son, by Tama M. Montgomery (Ideals Children's Books).

The parable of the prodigal son retold for children.

We Ask Forgiveness: A Young Child's Book for Reconciliation (St. Anthony Messenger Press).

A child's introduction to the Rite of Penance.

Books for Adults
The Reconciling Community: The Rite of Penance, by James Dallen (Liturgical Press).

A survey of the developments in sacramental theology and practice.

Your Child's First Confession: Preparing for the Sacrament of Reconciliation (Liguori).

An introduction to the sacrament for parents and families.

Multimedia for Children
Celebrating Our Faith (CD) (produced by GIA; BROWN-ROA).

One or more songs from this collection may be used to enhance classroom prayer and liturgy.

Celebrating Reconciliation with Children (6-part video series) (produced by Salt River Production Group; BROWN-ROA).

Segment 2: We Celebrate God's Love is designed for use with this chapter.

The Parable of the Prodigal Son (video) (produced by Twenty-Third Publications; BROWN-ROA).

A dramatization of Jesus' great parable of forgiveness.

Multimedia for Adults
Celebrating Reconciliation with Families (2-part video series) (produced by Salt River Production Group; BROWN-ROA).

Father Joe Kempf helps parents reflect on the meaning of the sacrament.

Pardon and Peace (video) (Franciscan Communications/St. Anthony Messenger Press).

WE ARE INVITED

1. Open

Gathering Invite the children to think of a time when they did something wrong or hurt someone else. Ask them to keep that experience in mind as you pray together the opening prayer.

Prayer Pray together the opening prayer. See *Music for Prayer* for suggested songs to accompany the opening prayer.

Working with the Pictures

Draw attention to the photograph on this page.

What do you think might have happened to cause these two sisters to be angry with each other? (Accept all reasonable responses.)

What can the girls do to make things right again? (Possible answers: They can say they are sorry; they can ask forgiveness; they can hug each other and go back to playing.)

Working with the Text

• Read the text aloud.

• Invite volunteers to answer the text question at the bottom of the page. (Possible answers: We might lose our friends and family members; we might be all alone; we might be sad forever.)

CHAPTER 2

WE CELEBRATE GOD'S LOVE

Dear God—Father, Son, and Holy Spirit— you are always ready to welcome us back. Help us turn to you with love and faithfulness. Amen!

Even in the most loving families, people do not always act lovingly. Even best friends sometimes hurt each other.

You know what it is like to do something wrong or hurt someone else. And you know what it is like to feel sorry and want to make up.

What if you never got a second chance?

14 : We Are Invited

Resource Center

Music for Prayer

If the children are learning a First Reconciliation song with the theme of God's forgiving love, sing it before or after the opening prayer. Other suggestions for music to enhance this prayer are "A Means of Your Peace," "Dona Nobis Pacem," or "I Want to Walk as a Child of Light" from the *Celebrating Our Faith* CD.

Teaching Tip

Handling sensitive topics Forgiveness can be a difficult topic for children who have been deeply hurt by someone they have trusted and loved. Emphasize that forgiveness and reconciliation are not always easy tasks. We need the Holy Spirit's help to be able to forgive those who have hurt us in serious ways. Even when we can't forgive someone because the hurt is too great, God never stops loving us and is always ready to forgive us.

It's a good thing that family members and friends almost always forgive one another. They **reconcile**, or come back together in peace.

When we **sin**, we do things that hurt our relationship with God and with others. We need a way to say we are sorry and that we want to do better. We need to ask forgiveness. We want a second chance.

God always loves us. God always offers us forgiveness. We accept God's forgiveness when we are sorry for our sins. We celebrate God's mercy in the Sacrament of **Reconciliation**.

We Are Invited : 15

Working with the Text

- Write the words *reconcile, sin,* and *Sacrament of Reconciliation* on the board. Underline *Reconciliation*. Tell the children that these are important words to know when we are sorry and want to ask for a second chance. Use *The Language of Faith* to clarify the meanings of the bold-faced terms.

- Read aloud or summarize the text on this page. Point out that God's forgiveness is always available to us when we ask for it.
  What do we call the special way the Church has of celebrating God's forgiveness?
  (the Sacrament of Reconciliation)

Working with the Pictures

- Direct attention to the photograph on this page. Invite volunteers to describe what they see in the picture.

- Help the children understand that the girl in the picture is celebrating the Sacrament of Reconciliation. The priest is celebrating the sacrament with her. He stands in the place of Jesus and offers God's forgiveness.

- Explain that the priest is pointing to the opened Bible because he probably has read a story of God's forgiveness to the girl who is celebrating Reconciliation. Hearing God's word in the Scriptures helps us be more sure that God is waiting to shower us with his forgiveness.

The Language of Faith

- To **reconcile** means to forgive one another and be at peace. When we reconcile with God and one another, we choose to come back into friendship. We are willing to make right whatever caused us to be separated from one another.

- **Sin** means to turn away from God and freely choose what is wrong. We can also sin when we choose not to do what we know is right.

- The Sacrament of **Reconciliation** is the Church's special way of helping us turn back to God and one another after we have chosen to sin. This sacrament celebrates God's forgiveness and renews our friendship with him.

Notes

Working with the Text

- Invite the children to find comfortable positions to share the Scripture story.

- Read aloud or retell the first part of the story found on this page. Use an engaging tone of voice to help the children picture the action of the story in their imaginations.

- After reading or retelling the first part of the story, discuss it with the children.
  What did the son want of his father? (his share of his father's money that some day would be his)
  What did the son do with all the money his father gave him? (He spent it all on parties.)
  What made the son realize the mistake he had made? (The pigs he was caring for were eating better than he was.)
  What did the son decide to do? (go back home and tell his father that he was sorry)

Working with the Pictures

Ask the children to point to the small picture at the bottom of this page. Invite volunteers to describe what they see.
How do you think the boy's parents felt as they watched him leaving? (Possible answers: sad, disappointed, afraid for him, confused.)

The Forgiving Father

Jesus told this story to explain the happiness that forgiveness brings.

A man had two sons. The younger son went to his father and said, "Someday everything you have will belong to my brother and me. I want my share now." So the father gave the younger son a lot of money.

The son moved to a faraway city. He spent all his money partying. Soon the son was poor, hungry, and homeless.

The only job the son could get was taking care of a farmer's pigs. He slept in the smelly barn. "These pigs have better food than I do," the son thought. "I should go home. Maybe if I tell my father how sorry I am, he'll let me work as one of his servants."

16 : We Remember

Resource Center

Scripture Background

The title *The Forgiving Father* replaces the former title and emphasis of *The Prodigal Son*, one of the most familiar of Jesus' parables. Most Scripture scholars today interpret the parable as a story about a father: a father who gives generously, who waits, who runs out to meet, who forgives, and who celebrates what was lost. Meant to teach the infinite and undeserved mercy and forgiveness of God for all sinners, the parable turns the tables on all that humans would expect of the father in the story.

Art Background

- The small illustration depicts the boy's parents seeing him off on his journey. This part of the parable reflects God's gift of free will. Through free will we can freely choose to love God or to turn our backs on him and our heritage.

- The illustration of the boy with the pigs is a reminder of how low the boy had gone. To Jesus' Jewish listeners, working with pigs— whose meat was considered religiously unclean—was the worst possible job; it made the person religiously unclean as well.

So the son set out for his home far away. While he was still on the road, the son saw his father running toward him with his arms open. The son fell to his knees. "Forgive me, Father," the son said. "I'm a sinner. I have hurt you and the whole family. I'm so sorry."

Before the son could even finish, the father hugged him joyfully. "Welcome home, my son!" he said. The father gave the son new clothes and threw a party for the whole neighborhood. "Rejoice with me," the father said to everyone. "It was like my son was dead and now he is alive again!"

—based on Luke 15:11–32

We Remember : 17

Working with the Text

- Continue reading aloud or retelling the remainder of the Scripture story found on this page.
- Invite the children to reflect on the story by answering these questions. **Whom did the son find running toward him on the road?** (his father) **Whom does the father represent in this story?** (God the Father) **Who is the son in this story?** (us, when we sin) **As members of the Church, how do we celebrate when we are sorry and return to God?** (with the Sacrament of Reconciliation)

Working with the Pictures

- Invite the children to study the illustration on this page. Invite volunteers to describe what they see. **What do you think the people in the background might be saying to one another?** (Possible answers: How could his father forgive him? What will happen now? Is the boy really sorry?)
- Point out to the children that most people listening to Jesus would not have expected this ending to the story. The father in the story did not behave toward his son in a way that most people would have behaved. Jesus tells this story of forgiveness to teach us that God is just as willing to take us back home as is the father in this story.

Art Background

The illustration depicts the son's return to his father, who gave him everything he asked for. The parable tells us that the father stops his son as the son confesses his wrongdoing and, instead, hurries to assure him that he has been restored to complete sonship. In the background can be seen the guests who were invited to come to the feast. How confused they must have been not to be witnessing a family argument and the disowning of a boy who disgraced his family and took up the ways of the Gentiles! Instead, a great feast was awaiting them, which included meat, a rare dish reserved for only the most important occasions.

Enrichment

Role-play the Scripture story Use or adapt the script on pages HA3–HA4 to act out the story. Suggestions for simple costumes and props can be found on page HA2.

Build *Continued*

Working with the Text

- Read or summarize the text on this page.

- Use *The Language of Faith* to clarify the meanings of the bold-faced terms.

- Emphasize that we sin only when we do something on purpose that we know is wrong. Mistakes and accidents are not sins because mistakes and accidents are never done on purpose.

- Be sure the children understand that, like the Eucharist, the Sacrament of Reconciliation is a sacrament they are invited to celebrate often throughout their lives.

Working with the Pictures

Direct attention to the photograph on this page. Explain that this is a communal celebration of the sacrament, or the way the sacrament is celebrated with the community present. Invite the children to look closely at the picture's background to see some of the other people celebrating this sacrament, too. Then explain that the girl in the picture is telling her sins to the priest and the priest will help her find ways to avoid these sins in the future. Stress that this part of the celebration is always private.

Our Second Chance

Baptism takes away **original sin** and all personal sin. But because we are human, we are tempted to do what is wrong. We have **free will**, like the son in Jesus' story. We can choose to sin. The Sacrament of Reconciliation gives us a chance to ask God's forgiveness and promise to do better.

Baptism, the first sacrament, is a once-in-a-lifetime sacrament. The Sacrament of Reconciliation can be celebrated at any time, again and again throughout our lives. Reconciliation is necessary in the case of serious sin. It is helpful even in the case of less serious sin.

Resource Center

The Language of Faith

- ***Original sin*** is the sinful condition into which we are born. This condition came from the first humans' choice to disobey God. Baptism restores the relationship of loving grace lost through original sin.

- The gift of ***free will*** allows us to choose between good and evil. Humans are the only creatures of God who have been given this special gift. God does not force us against our wills to love what is good but gives us the freedom to make that decision for ourselves.

Teaching Tip

Handling sensitive topics Sometimes children of this age are very willing to discuss their sins with everyone. Emphasize that although everyone sins from time to time, a person's sins are very private and should not be discussed with just anyone. Assure them that the priest who celebrates the Sacrament of Reconciliation is not allowed to discuss their sins with anyone, not even their family members. On the other hand, if something the children have said or done is upsetting them and they would feel better talking to someone about it, then they shouldn't hesitate to speak in confidence to a family member or trusted adult.

We almost always celebrate Reconciliation in two different ways. In **individual** celebrations a person called a **penitent** meets with a priest in private. In **communal** celebrations groups of people gather to pray and listen to readings from the Bible. Then each person speaks privately with a priest.

Whichever way we celebrate, the priest does not forgive our sins. Only God can forgive sins. The priest acts in the name of Jesus, who shows us God's forgiving love. Like the father in Jesus' story, the priest welcomes us back home to our Catholic community.

We Ask

What is the difference between mortal sin and venial sin?

Serious sin is called **mortal**, or "deadly." It cuts us off from God's grace and friendship. For sin to be mortal, it must be seriously wrong, we must know it is seriously wrong, and we must freely choose to do it anyway. **Venial** sin is less serious, but it still hurts our relationship with God and others. *(Catechism, #1855–1857)*

We Celebrate : 19

We Celebrate

Build *Continued*

Working with the Text

- Read the text aloud. Write the words *individual* and *communal* on the board. Use *The Language of Faith* to clarify the meanings of these two terms and the term *penitent*.

- Help the children discuss the text with these questions.
  Who shows us God's forgiving love and welcomes us back home to our Catholic community in the Sacrament of Reconciliation? (the priest)
  Who is the only one who can forgive sins? (God)

Working with the Pictures

Ask the children to look at the photograph on this page.
What does the baptismal font remind us of? (our Baptism)
How is the Sacrament of Reconciliation like the Sacrament of Baptism? (Both sacraments forgive sins.)

We Ask Invite a volunteer to read the question aloud. Then read the answer aloud to the children. Pause often to check their understanding. Assure the children that at their ages it is highly unlikely that they are capable of mortal, or serious, sin. Yet all sins damage our friendship with God and others. When we are sorry, we should reconcile with God and the person we've hurt as soon as possible.

The Language of Faith

- **Individual** means "by oneself." When we celebrate the Sacrament of Reconciliation as individuals, we approach the priest to ask God's forgiveness at a time when the rest of the community is not present. Parishes usually have certain times during the week or on weekends for individual celebrations of this sacrament.

- The **penitent** is the person confessing sin, accepting a penance, and seeking absolution in the Sacrament of Reconciliation.

- **Communal** celebrations of the Sacrament of Reconciliation usually take place in parishes during the Seasons of Advent and Lent. At these celebrations the community gathers. Together the members of the community pray, listen to Scripture readings, and privately examine their consciences. During the celebration they confess their sins to a priest in private.

Multicultural Link

Catholics are not the only people who practice forgiveness and reconciliation, although the Sacrament of Reconciliation as we understand it is not practiced in most faith traditions. Forgiveness and reconciliation is the call of Jesus to all his followers. All Christians, as followers of Jesus, are required to live lives of pardon and reconciliation. The Jewish people set aside one special day each year, called *Yom Kippur*, to confess their sins to God and make atonement for them.

WE LIVE RECONCILIATION

3. Close

Working with the Page

- Read the directions aloud. Allow the children time to think about what they will draw or write in the heart.

- Provide writing and art materials. Play quiet music to accompany the children's work. This page may also be assigned as a take-home activity.

- Encourage the children to share their completed work now or during a later session.

Living Reconciliation at Home

Suggest this follow-up activity.

- With your family, spend a few minutes this week thanking God for his gifts of free will, forgiveness, and peace. To end the prayer time, extend a sign of peace to each family member.

Living Reconciliation in the Parish

Distribute copies of *My Reconciliation Book* booklets, if you have not already done so. Explain to the children that they will be using these booklets throughout their preparation for First Reconciliation and may continue to use them whenever they celebrate the sacrament thereafter. Have the children complete these activities in class or at home with family members or prayer partners.

- Complete the information on page 1 of *My Reconciliation Book*, and read and color page 2.

- Find out when your parish has scheduled times for individual celebrations of Reconciliation.

Getting Ready for First Reconciliation

Have the children work in small groups to discuss this question.

Doing anything for the first time can make us nervous or frightened. Celebrating Reconciliation for the first time might be one of those experiences. What can you do to remind yourself that this is a celebration of God's forgiveness and peace and not a time to worry or be afraid?

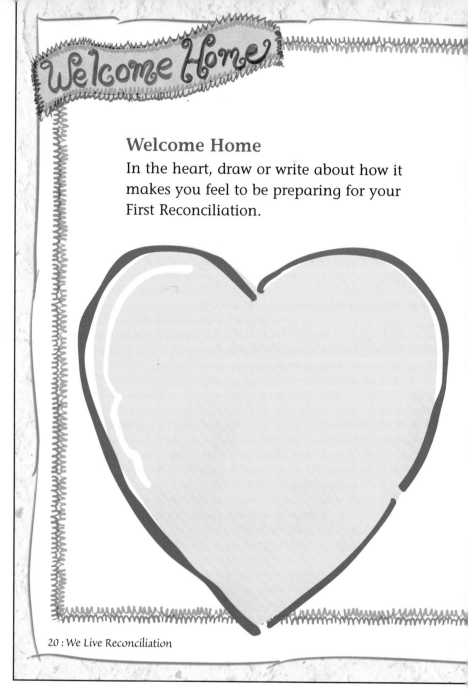

Welcome Home

In the heart, draw or write about how it makes you feel to be preparing for your First Reconciliation.

20 : We Live Reconciliation

Resource Center

Link to the Family

Distribute the Chapter 2 *Sharing Page* to be taken home. Encourage the children to take their books and Reconciliation booklets home to share with family members.

Link to Liturgy

Take the children on a tour of the parish Reconciliation room or confessional. Demonstrate the various ways your parish celebrates the sacrament individually and communally.

We Ask God's Blessing

In the Sacrament of Reconciliation,
we are all welcomed home by our
forgiving Father.

May the Father bless us,
for he has adopted us as his children.
Amen!
May the Son come to help us,
for he has welcomed us as brothers
and sisters.
Amen!
May the Spirit be with us,
for he has made his home in us.
Amen!

—based on the Rite of Penance

WELCOME HOME!

We Live Reconciliation : 21

Working with the Page

- Spend a few minutes looking
  back through this chapter with
  the children. Ask the children to
  comment on their favorite parts
  of the lesson.
- Direct the children's attention to
  the symbols that make up the
  page border. Invite volunteers to
  explain the connection between
  the symbols and the chapter theme.
  (The *Welcome Home* signs are
  reminders of the story of the
  Forgiving Father and symbols
  of Reconciliation.)
- Have the children bring their books
  to the classroom prayer space or
  the church. Gather around a table
  or in the Reconciliation room.
  If possible, have the children's
  families and their prayer partners
  join you for the prayer.

Prayer Lead the children in the
prayer, beginning and ending
with the Sign of the Cross. See
Music for Prayer for suggested songs
to accompany this closing prayer.

Music for Prayer

To enhance the prayer celebration, you may wish
to have the children sing a musical setting of the
Great Amen used at Mass in your parish. Other
songs that may accompany this closing prayer are
"Rain Down," "You Are Mine," or a song from the
Celebrating Our Faith CD.

Notes

_____
_____
_____
_____
_____
_____

WE HEAR GOOD NEWS

Key Content Summary

The Scriptures are God's good news for us. When we read and share God's word, God himself is with us, offering mercy and forgiveness. The Scriptures are an important part of the celebration of Reconciliation.

Planning the Chapter

Open	Pacing Guide *Suggested time/Your time*	Content	Objectives	Materials
	10–20 min./ ____ min.	We Are Invited, pp. 22–23	• Recognize the importance of sharing good news.	• music for prayer (optional)

Build				
	35–45 min./ ____ min.	We Remember, pp. 24–25	• Recall Jesus' parable of the lost sheep, with its good news of God's forgiveness.	• copies of the script on pages HA6–HA7, simple costumes and props (optional)
		We Celebrate, pp. 26–27	• Identify the ways we hear God's good news in the Scriptures. • Describe the role of the Scriptures in the celebration of Reconciliation.	

Close				
	15 min./ ____ min.	We Live Reconciliation, pp. 28–29	• Celebrate the good news of God's love.	• writing materials • *My Reconciliation Book* • Chapter 3 *Sharing Page* • music for prayer (optional) • construction paper, writing and drawing materials (optional)

Catechism Background

See Catechism of the Catholic Church, #104, 1349.

Doctrinal Foundation   We meet God in the Scriptures. The inspired word of God is a living presence in the Christian community. In some form the word is shared in the celebration of each sacrament. The message of the Scriptures has special meaning in the context of Reconciliation. By reflecting on God's word, we measure our choices against the call to holiness. "Your word is a lamp that gives light wherever I walk" *(Psalm 119:105)*. We are reminded of the law of love. "Our Lord, your love is seen all over the world. Teach me your laws" *(Psalm 119:64)*. And we are encouraged to turn in contrition to the Lord, who is "kind and patient and always loving" *(Psalm 145:8)*.

One-Minute Retreat

Read

"The word of God which you receive by your ear, hold fast in your heart. For the word of God is the food of the soul."

—*Saint Gregory the Great*

Reflect

How well do I listen to God's good news in the Scriptures?

How can reflecting on God's word help me avoid sin and seek forgiveness?

Pray

God of kindness and mercy,
you have given me your word as a beacon for my
    journey.
Help me share the light of the gospel
with the children
as they prepare to celebrate your loving forgiveness
in the Sacrament of Reconciliation.
Amen.

Library Links

Books for Children

The Lord Is My Shepherd: The 23rd Psalm, by Tasha Tudor (Philomel Books).

A beautifully illustrated version of the beloved psalm for children.

The Lost Sheep, by Debbie Tafton O'Neal (Judson Press).

A retelling of Jesus' parable about God's mercy.

Books for Adults

How to Read and Pray the Gospel (Liguori).

A handbook for living God's word every day.

"What the Gospels Say About Conversion," by Ronald D. Witherup SS (*Catholic Update*; St. Anthony Messenger Press).

Multimedia for Children

Celebrating Our Faith (CD) (produced by GIA; BROWN-ROA).

One or more songs from this CD may be used to enhance classroom prayer and liturgy.

Celebrating Reconciliation with Children (6-part video series) (produced by Salt River Production Group; BROWN-ROA).

Segment 3: *We Hear Good News* is designed for use with this chapter.

"Let the Children Come to Me": The Word of God Alive for Children (video) (Liguori).

A child's introduction to Scripture.

The Parable of the Lost Sheep (video) (produced by Twenty-Third Publications; BROWN-ROA).

Jesus' story of God's mercy is dramatized for children.

Multimedia for Adults

Liturgy: Becoming the Word of God (audio) (Franciscan Communications/St. Anthony Messenger Press).

Popular lecturer Megan McKenna speaks about living God's word.

WE ARE INVITED

1. Open

Gathering Invite the children to think of a time when they received good news. Invite volunteers to share their experiences. If time permits, share an experience of good news that you've had.

Prayer Pray the opening prayer together. See *Music for Prayer* for suggested songs to accompany the opening prayer.

Working with the Pictures

Ask the children to look carefully at the photograph on this page. **Why do you think the first place award was good news for this family?** (Possible answers: They are happy that their son is using his talents; they are proud of the boy's work; he had been working very hard to win this prize.)

Working with the Text

Read the text aloud. **Why is good news fun to share?** (Possible answers: It makes people happy to hear good news; it feels good to be able to tell good news.)

CHAPTER 3

WE HEAR GOOD NEWS

Dear God—Father, Son, and Holy Spirit— you give us the good news of your love. Help us understand your word and live by it. Amen!

What's the best news you have ever heard?

Maybe you found out you were going to have a brother or sister. Maybe your dog had puppies, or you found out your favorite relative was coming to visit for a week.

What did you do when you heard the news? Most people want to tell someone else right away. Good news is meant to be shared.

22 : We Are Invited

Resource Center

Music for Prayer

Some suggestions for music to enhance this prayer are "Come, Lord Jesus," "Send Us Your Spirit," "Wa Wa Wa Emimimo," or "Shepherd Me, O God" from the *Celebrating Our Faith* CD.

Enrichment

Role-playing Encourage the children to role-play situations in which people hear good news. Have them work in pairs or small groups to make up the situation and the dialogue. Provide sufficient time for the pairs or groups to role play their good news scenarios for the class.

Notes

God has good news for us. God our Father sent his Son, Jesus, to bring us the good news of his love and forgiveness. We hear this good news whenever we hear or read the words of **Scripture**, found in the Bible.

God's good news is especially important to share when we are feeling sorry for sin. Readings from the Bible are part of our celebration of the Sacrament of Reconciliation. God's good news gives us the hope and courage we need to start again.

We Are Invited : 23

Working with the Text

• Read aloud or summarize the text on this page. Use *The Language of Faith* to clarify the meaning of the bold-faced word.

• Invite the children to discuss the text.
What good news does God have for us? (that he loves and forgives us)
Who brought that good news to us? (Jesus, God's Son)
When is it especially important for us to hear God's good news? (when we are feeling sorry for having sinned)

• Emphasize that God's good news can bring us the hope and encouragement to start over when we have sinned and turned away from God.

Working with the Pictures

• Direct attention to the photograph of the boy celebrating Reconciliation. **What do you think the boy and priest are sharing?** (God's good news found in the Scriptures)

• Explain to the children that sometimes the Scriptures are shared with us when we celebrate individual Reconciliation. The priest may recite some verses from Scripture or invite us to read from the Bible. The Scriptures are always shared with us when we celebrate communal Reconciliation.

The Language of Faith

The words of **Scripture** are God's word of good news, written down for us in the sacred book called the *Bible*. The word *scripture* comes from the Latin word *scriptus*, which means "writing." Catholics believe that God speaks to us in the Scriptures, which were inspired by the Holy Spirit.

Multicultural Link

Explain to the children that many religious traditions have writings that they consider to be God's word for them. All these writings may be called *scripture* because they are considered by them to be sacred writings. The Jewish people share most of the same books of the Old Testament that Christians hold as sacred. Muslims call their holy book the *Qur'an*, which they believe contains God's word to their holy leader, Muhammad. Point out to the children that most religious traditions believe that God communicates with them through their holy books, which are to be read and shared often.

2. Build

Working with the Text

- Invite the children to find comfortable positions for sharing the Scripture story.

- Read aloud or retell the part of the story found on this page. Use an engaging tone of voice to draw the children into the excitement of the story.

- Help the children reflect on the story by discussing it with them. **Why did the shepherd ask for help?** (One of his sheep was missing, and he wanted to find it.) **Did his friends think this was a good idea?** (No, because it was only one sheep and the shepherd still had ninety-nine others.) **Why did the shepherd want to find the one that was lost?** (because that sheep was lost and afraid and needed the shepherd the most)

One Lost Sheep

People sometimes asked Jesus why he spent so much time with sinners. Shouldn't he be bringing the good news of God's love to holy people? Jesus answered them with a story.

Once there was a shepherd who took care of a hundred sheep. Every night before closing the gate to the sheep pen, the shepherd counted his sheep.

One night there were only ninety-nine. The shepherd counted again. Still only ninety-nine! Where could the missing sheep be?

The shepherd called all his friends to help him look. "Why bother?" one friend asked. "It's only one lost sheep. You've got ninety-nine safe here to take care of!"

"It's the one lost sheep who needs me most," the shepherd said. Then he and his friends looked everywhere a wandering sheep might hide.

Finally, the shepherd found his one lost sheep. It was curled up under a bush, tired and frightened. The shepherd put the sheep on his shoulders.

24 : We Remember

Resource Center

Scripture Background

The image of the shepherd is found throughout the Old and New Testaments. In the New Testament all four Gospels contain images of Jesus as the Good Shepherd. The Good Shepherd watches over the sheep entrusted to him with the care and tenderness of a shepherd willing to lay down his life for his sheep. In Paul's Letter to the **Ephesians**, in the **Acts of the Apostles**, and in the **First Letter of Peter**, the term *shepherd* is applied to the leaders and elders of the Church. Today, *pastor*, the Latin word for "shepherd," is used to describe the ordained leaders of a diocese or parish.

He called out to his friends, "Stop searching! I've found the sheep that was lost!"

The shepherd and his friends sang as they brought the lost sheep home. They woke up all ninety-nine other sheep with their shouts of joy!

—*based on Luke 15:1–7*

We Remember : 25

Working with the Text

Continue reading aloud or retelling the Scripture story found on this page. Talk with the children about the ending.
Did the shepherd find his lost sheep? (yes)
How did the shepherd feel about finding his one lost sheep?
(He was very happy and sang and shouted with joy.)

Working with the Pictures

• Draw attention to the illustration on pages 24–25. Invite volunteers to describe what they see.

• Remind the children that sheep and shepherds were a common sight in Jesus' homeland. It was the job of a hired shepherd to keep the sheep safe from wild animals or from people who might try to steal them.
Jesus is our Good Shepherd. How does Jesus try to keep us safe from harm?
(Possible answers: He tells us about God's love and forgiveness; he sends us people who love and care for us; he lives in our hearts, keeping us close to him always.)

Art Background

The art on this page shows the image of a shepherd carrying his lost sheep back to the fold while other shepherds look on. The shepherd was scorned by most people in society because he was a wanderer, a nomad, who would leave his wife and children for months at a time to follow his sheep from one pasture to another. The shepherd and his sheep were often thrown off a property because of the damage the sheep would do to the pasture land. It was a lowly job that paid little and brought little respect, yet Jesus chose to use this image to describe himself and his faithfulness to his "flock," the people entrusted to him by God the Father. The image of Jesus as a Good Shepherd is one of the earliest images of Jesus in religious art.

Enrichment

Role-play the Scripture story Use or adapt the script on pages HA6–HA7 to act out the story. Suggestions for simple costumes and props are found on page HA5.

Working with the Text

• Read aloud the text on this page.

• Write the terms *Gospels* and *Celebration of the Word of God* on the board. After the word *Gospels,* put an equal sign (=), and then write the words *good news.* Explain that the Gospels are the most important books of the Bible for Christians because they describe Jesus' life and teachings. The Gospels share God's good news with us.
Whose word is shared with us during the Celebration of the Word of God? (God's word)
Why do you think we share God's word as a part of the celebration of every sacrament? (God's word brings us the good news that we are loved and forgiven.)

Working with the Pictures

Ask the children to look at the photograph on this page. Help them recognize it as a part of the Sacrament of Reconciliation called the *Celebration of the Word of God.*
What should we do during the Celebration of the Word of God? (We should listen carefully to God's word for us.)
How can you tell that the people in this photograph are listening carefully to the reader? (They are looking at her and sitting quietly.)

Words of Love and Mercy

Jesus' story about the lost sheep reminds us how much God loves us and wants to forgive us. This story, and many others, can be found in the **Gospels**, the books of the Bible that tell about Jesus' life and teachings. The word **gospel** means "good news."

Readings from the Bible are part of the celebration of every sacrament. We call this the **Celebration of the Word of God**.

We share stories from the Bible as part of the Sacrament of Reconciliation. These words of love and mercy help us see where we have sinned and how we can do better.

26 : We Celebrate

Resource Center

Link to Liturgy

The **Celebration of the Word of God** begins with a reading that is usually taken from the Old Testament. Following the first reading is an opportunity for the assembly to respond to God's word. We call this response the *Responsorial Psalm*. Then a second reading is shared, taken from one of the letters, or epistles, found in the New Testament. Finally, the gospel is read, as the assembly stands to welcome Jesus in the word of God proclaimed. The presiding priest or deacon shares a teaching about the readings with us. This special talk, called a *homily*, helps us understand God's word today and how to live it in this time and this place. The last part of the Celebration of the Word of God is the Penitential Intercessions. During this time of intercessory prayer, we respond to God's word by asking God to assist those who need help and consolation.

In a communal celebration of Reconciliation, we begin by singing a hymn. We pray that God will open our hearts so that we can ask forgiveness. Then we hear one or more readings from the Bible. The priest helps us understand what we have heard.

When we celebrate Reconciliation individually, the priest may read or have us read a few words from the Bible when we first get together. The message of Scripture starts us on our celebration of God's forgiving love.

Scripture is God's own word. When we hear or read the Bible as part of the Sacrament of Reconciliation, we are hearing God's message for us. In a communal celebration of Reconciliation, the priest's **homily** helps us understand the readings and apply them to our lives. In an individual celebration the priest and the penitent may discuss the Scripture reading together. *(Catechism, #104, 1349)*

We Celebrate : 27

WE CELEBRATE
Build *Continued*
Working with the Text

- Read aloud the text on this page.
- Tell the children that often we may not understand the reading from Scripture because the experience happened in another place and in another time, very different from our own. Point out to the children the importance of having a priest or deacon explain God's word.
- Invite the children to respond to these questions.
  What do we pray for at the beginning of a communal celebration of Reconciliation? (that God will open our hearts so we can ask forgiveness)
  How does the message of Scripture help us? (It starts us on our celebration of God's forgiving love.)

Working with the Pictures

- Draw attention to the photograph of the priest giving a homily. Invite volunteers to describe what they see in the picture. (a priest giving a homily at a children's Mass or communal Reconciliation service)

We Ask Invite a volunteer to read the question aloud. Then read the answer aloud, pausing often to ensure the children's understanding. Use *The Language of Faith* to help clarify the meaning of *homily*. Point out the importance of knowing what God is saying to us today.

The Language of Faith

The word **homily** comes from the Greek word meaning "conversation" or "speech." The homily, in the past known as a sermon, is a special talk, or speech, given by the presiding priest or deacon during the Celebration of the Word of God. Its main purpose is to explain the Scriptures, especially the gospel, and how to apply it to our lives.

Teaching Tip

Explaining the role of the homilist Help the children understand that the ordained ministers in the Church have a special duty to teach and explain the Scriptures and all the teachings of the Church and help us apply them in our lives. They are our special teachers, who help us know more about God's love for us. As a teacher the presiding priest or deacon teaches or explains what the Bible readings mean. Tell the children that this special talk, called the *homily*, is given by an ordained minister.

3. Close

Working with the Page

- Write on the board the following Bible verses or a few of your own choosing.

  "You, Lord, are my shepherd. I will never be in need" *(Psalm 23:1)*.

  "Nothing can separate us from God's love" *(Romans 8:38)*.

  "Always be glad because of the Lord!" *(Philippians 4:4)*.

- Read the directions to the activity aloud. Invite volunteers to read the Scripture verses you wrote on the board. Give the children time to choose one of the verses.

- Provide writing materials, and give the children time to copy onto the bookmark the Bible verse they chose.

- Encourage the children to share the Bible verse they wrote on their bookmarks with their family members and prayer partners.

Living Reconciliation at Home

Suggest this follow-up activity.

- Make a Scripture bookmark for someone who is ill, alone, or hurting. Give the bookmark to the person as a sign of your love for him or her.

Living Reconciliation in the Parish

Have the children complete these activities in class or at home with family members or prayer partners.

- Color pages 3–5 and 11–12 of *My Reconciliation Book*.

- Listen to the Scripture readings and the homily at Mass this week. What do they tell you about how God wants you to live?

Getting Ready for First Reconciliation

Have the children work in small groups to discuss this question.

Soon you will celebrate the Sacrament of Reconciliation for the first time. How can God's word in the Bible help you get ready for this special celebration?

Words to Live By

Your teacher will write some Bible verses on the board. Choose your favorite, and copy it onto the bookmark.

_____

_____

_____

_____

_____

_____

_____

_____

28 : We Live Reconciliation

Resource Center

Link to the Family

Distribute the Chapter 3 *Sharing Page* to be taken home. Encourage the children to take their books and Reconciliation booklets home to share with family members.

Link to Liturgy

Pages 3–5 and 11–12 of *My Reconciliation Book* cover the introductory prayers and sharing of Scripture in communal and individual celebrations of the sacrament. Review these parts of the Rite of Penance with the children, reading the prayers aloud, helping the children memorize the responses, and practicing any gestures or postures.

The Lord Is Good!

We thank God for the good news of his love.

Shout praises to the LORD, everyone on
   this earth.
Be joyful and sing as you come in to
   worship the LORD!
The LORD is good!
His love and faithfulness will last forever.
You know the LORD is God!
He created us, and we belong to him;
   we are his people, the sheep in his pasture.
The LORD is good!
His love and faithfulness will last forever.
Be thankful and praise the LORD
   as you enter his temple.
The LORD is good!
His love and faithfulness will last forever.

—Psalm 100

We Live Reconciliation : 29

Working with the Page

- Spend a few moments looking
  back through this chapter with the
  children. Invite volunteers to point
  out their favorite parts of the lesson.
- Draw the children's attention to the
  symbols that make up the page
  border. Invite volunteers to explain
  the connection between these
  symbols and the chapter theme.
  (The sheep and shepherd crooks
  remind us of Jesus' Parable of the
  Lost Sheep.)
- Have the children bring their books
  to the classroom prayer space or
  the church. Gather around a table
  or the ambo. If possible, have the
  children's families and their prayer
  partners join you for the prayer.

Prayer   Teach the children the
response to the prayer on this page:
"The Lord is good! His love and
faithfulness will last forever."
Lead the children in the prayer,
beginning and ending with the
Sign of the Cross. See *Music for Prayer*
for suggested songs to accompany
this closing prayer.

Music for Prayer

To enhance the prayer celebration, you may wish
to use one of the following songs: "Come, Worship
the Lord," "Lift Up Your Hearts," or a song from the
Celebrating Our Faith CD.

Enrichment

Make a Scripture triptych   Provide the children
with art and writing materials. Have each child fold
a large sheet of construction paper into thirds.
Brainstorm with the children some of their favorite
Bible stories. Then have the children choose one of
those stories to illustrate. They should draw one part
of the story on each third of the paper. Provide time
for the children to share their completed work with
the class.

Notes

WE LOOK AT OUR LIVES

Key Content Summary

True happiness comes from doing what God wants us to do. The Ten Commandments sum up God's law and are in turn summarized by the Great Commandment. As part of the process of conversion, we examine our consciences, measuring our actions against God's law as revealed in the Scriptures, the teachings of the Church, and the life of Jesus.

Planning the Chapter

	Pacing Guide *Suggested time/Your time*	Content	Objectives	Materials
Open	10–20 min./ ___ min.	We Are Invited, pp. 30–31	• Recognize that true happiness comes from following God's commandments.	• music for prayer (optional)
Build	35–45 min./ ___ min.	We Remember, pp. 32–33	• Recall the giving of the Ten Commandments and Jesus' teaching about the Great Commandment.	
		We Celebrate, pp. 34–35	• Identify the steps in examining one's conscience. • Describe the role of examination of conscience in the Sacrament of Reconciliation.	• art materials for bracelets, buttons, bookmarks, wallet cards, or stickers (optional)
Close	15 min./ ___ min.	We Live Reconciliation, pp. 36–37	• Celebrate the help of the Holy Spirit.	• writing and drawing materials • *My Reconciliation Book* • Chapter 4 *Sharing Page* • music for prayer (optional)

Catechism Background

Doctrinal Foundation   At various times in our lives we may think of conscience as an external, friendly voice that consistently nudges us in the correct moral direction. The truth, of course, is more wonderfully complex. Conscience may indeed be thought of as a voice, but it is an internal voice, a harmony of intellect and reason, emotion and will knitted into our personhood by God. And in order to rely on the nudgings of that voice, we must take the responsibility of forming our conscience, nurturing it on the law as revealed to us in the Scriptures, in the teachings of the Church, and in the person of Jesus. Fortunately, we have the help of the Holy Spirit. "Our Lord, you bless everyone who lives right and obeys your Law. You bless all those who follow your commands from deep in their hearts" *(Psalm 119:1–2)*.

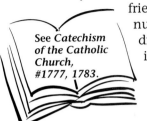

See *Catechism of the Catholic Church,* #1777, 1783.

One-Minute Retreat

Read

"What we call conscience is the voice of Divine Love in the deep of our being, desiring union with our will."

—J. P. Greaves

Reflect

What image do I have of my conscience?
How do I nourish and form my conscience?

Pray

God of Wisdom,
open my mind and heart to your will,
and shape my conscience with your love.
Send your Spirit to guide the children
as they grow in understanding.
Help us all make the good and loving choices
you call us to make.
Amen.

Library Links

Books for Children
We Ask Forgiveness: A Young Child's Book for Reconciliation (St. Anthony Messenger Press).
   Includes material on examining one's conscience.

Books for Adults
Living the Ten Commandments: A Positive Approach, by Marilyn Gustin (Liguori).
   The commandments as positive guidelines, not negative proscriptions.

Making a Better Confession: A Deeper Examination of Conscience, by Con O'Connell OFM (Liguori).
   Going beyond the formula to real conversion.

"Your Conscience and Church Teaching: How Do They Fit Together?" by Nicholas Lohkamp OFM (*Catholic Update*; St. Anthony Messenger Press).

Multimedia for Children
Celebrating Our Faith (CD) (produced by GIA; BROWN-ROA).
   One or more songs from this collection may be used to enhance classroom prayer and liturgy.

Celebrating Reconciliation with Children (6-part video series) (produced by Salt River Production Group; BROWN-ROA).
   Segment 4: We Look at Our Lives is designed for use with this chapter.

Kevin's Temptation (video) (produced by Twenty-Third Publications; BROWN-ROA).
   A story about making the right choice.

Moses the Lawgiver (video) (produced by Rabbit Ears Productions; BROWN-ROA).
   The story of the Ten Commandments.

One Good Turn: Making a Moral Decision (video) (produced by Barbara Bartley; BROWN-ROA).
   Suggestions for making and evaluating moral choices.

Multimedia for Adults
Making Sense of Christian Morality (4-part video series) (Franciscan Communications/St. Anthony Messenger Press).
   Paulist Father Richard Sparks addresses key issues of Christian moral formation.

Seven Principles for Teaching Christian Morality (audio) (Franciscan Communications/St. Anthony Messenger Press).
   Tips for parents and catechists.

WE ARE INVITED

1. Open

Gathering   Ask the children to think of times when they have been very happy. Invite volunteers to describe some of those special times.

Prayer   Pray the opening prayer together. See *Music for Prayer* for suggested songs to accompany the opening prayer.

Working with the Pictures

Direct attention to the photograph of the happy children on this page. Ask the children to describe what they see.
Why do you think these children are happy? (Possible answers: They like having their pictures taken; they are having fun playing together; it's a special day at school; they have just heard good news.)

Working with the Text

• Read the text aloud. Give volunteers the opportunity to suggest what makes them really happy.

• Talk with the children about true happiness. Emphasize that it is the people we share our lives with who make us really happy.
Who in your life makes you really happy? (Possible answers: my mom and dad, my friends, my brothers and sisters, my grandparents.)

CHAPTER 4

WE LOOK AT OUR LIVES

Dear God—Father, Son, and Holy Spirit— you call us to be happy with you forever. Help us live by our covenant of love with you. Amen!

What makes you happy? Real happiness comes from sharing love, friendship, and good times.

   God made each person to be really happy forever. We are most happy when we are living the way God made us to live.

30 : We Are Invited

Resource Center

Teaching Tip

Handling sensitive topics   Point out to the class that it's OK not to feel happy all the time. Sometimes we need to feel sad or angry because of what is going on in our lives. Tell the children that it's OK to have these feelings.

Music for Prayer

Suggestions for music to enhance this prayer are "Only Your Love," "Hold Us in Your Mercy," or "A Means of Your Peace" from the *Celebrating Our Faith* CD.

Notes

God loves us so much. He gave us the **commandments** as a sign of his love. The commandments show us how to live as God wants us to live. They tell us how to love God and others. The commandments show us the way to real happiness.

We Are Invited : 31

Working with the Text

• Write the word *commandments* on the board next to the words *the way to real happiness*. Add an equal sign (=) to connect the two sets of words.

• Tell the children that other names for commandments are *rules* or *laws*. Write these words under the word *commandments*.

• Read the text aloud, or summarize it in your own words.
Why does God want us to be happy? (because God loves us)
What happens to us and to our world when we don't live the way that God made us to live? (Possible answers: We are not happy; others are not happy.)

Working with the Pictures

• Direct attention to the photograph on this page. Invite volunteers to suggest what might have just happened between the boy and his father. (Possible answers: They have just made up; the father is telling the boy how happy he is with him; they are saying that they love each other and want each other to be happy.)

• Point out to the children that when we love someone, we want that person to be happy. God loves us very much and wants us to be happy. To help us be really happy, God gave us the commandments.

Catechetical Background

It is not necessary for children this age to memorize the Ten Commandments. However, you may wish to refer the children to the Ten Commandments on page 57 and use this reference to explain what the commandments require of us. Tell the children that Jesus lived by these same commandments, or special laws of God, and that we are called to live according to them as a sign of our friendship with God.

The Language of Faith

The **commandments** are rules of living given by God to Moses on Mount Sinai. The Ten Commandments, the most familiar of these rules, tell us how we are to live in a holy relationship with God and others. The first three commandments describe how we are to love God. The next seven commandments describe how we are to treat ourselves and others. Both Jews and Christians strive to live by these commandments.

Working with the Pictures

- Draw attention to the illustration of Moses and the Ten Commandments. Invite volunteers to describe what they see in the picture.

- Tell the children that the man holding the two stone tablets is Moses, a friend of God and an important leader of the people of Israel. Explain that Moses lived many, many years before Jesus. **What message from God do you think Moses will have for the people of Israel?** (Possible answers: Tell the people that I love them; tell them that I want them to love others.)

Working with the Text

- Invite the children to find comfortable positions for listening to the Scripture story.

- Read aloud or retell the story on this page. Emphasize that the people of Israel understood that the commandments were God's word for them. These laws of God became very important in their lives. **What was the covenent that God entered into with the people of Israel?** (a promise of lasting love) Tell the children that God made a covenant with them. Help them understand that at Baptism we become children of God, followers of Jesus, and members of the Church family. We enter into a lasting promise of love with God.

The Great Commandment

God made a **covenant**, a lasting promise of love, with the people of Israel. God gave their leader, Moses, the commandments as a sign of the covenant. The Ten Commandments were carved on stone tablets.

But the commandments were not just laws written on stone. The people kept these words in their hearts. They honored them in their lives.

32 : We Remember

Resource Center

Scripture Background

The story of the giving of the Ten Commandments to Moses by God is found in the **Book of Exodus** and in the **Book of Deuteronomy**. The God of the Israelites would live in a special relationship with his people. As a sign of the **covenant**, or holy agreement, the Israelites would accept these special commandments. Living according to these laws would bring them true happiness. The laws of God were understood to be God's way of showing his love for them, because the laws helped them achieve true happiness.

One day when Jesus was teaching in a small town, a man who studied the commandments asked Jesus a question.

"What must I do to be happy forever with God?" he asked.

Jesus answered with a question of his own. "When you study God's law," Jesus asked, "what does it tell you?"

The student smiled. He said, "Love God with all your heart, with all your being, with all your strength, and with all your mind, and love your neighbor as you love yourself."

Jesus smiled, too. "That is the **Great Commandment**!" he said. "Do this, and you will live forever with God."

—based on Luke 10:25–28

We Remember : 33

Working with the Text

- Read aloud the Scripture story on this page. Remind the children that this story takes place many, many years after Moses accepted the commandments from God. Use *The Language of Faith* to further explain the *Great Commandment*.

- Invite the children to pause and reflect on this story.
  What question did the man ask Jesus? ("What must I do to be happy forever with God?")
  How did Jesus answer him? (Jesus asked the man to tell him what God's law says.)
  What *does* God's law say? (Love God with your whole self and love others as yourself.)
  What do we call this special law of God? (the Great Commandment)

Working with the Pictures

Draw attention to the illustration on this page.
Why do you think the other people shown in the illustration gathered around to hear Jesus? (Possible answers: They also wanted to know how to be happy forever with God; they wanted to see if Jesus knew the real answer.)
The man told Jesus what God's law said. How does God's law make us really happy? (God gave us the law out of love for us. He knew that if we lived by the law, we would be happy forever.)

Scripture Background

It was Jewish custom to debate the meaning of the Scriptures and to test Jewish leaders on their knowledge and wisdom. This story from Luke's Gospel is an example of this type of testing. Aware that he was being tested and that the man already knew the answer to his own question, Jesus allowed the man to answer it. The man repeats the heart of God's law—not the law as a set of rules to be followed, but rather as a way to live and love and find true happiness. Loving God and others is what is necessary to live with God forever.

The Language of Faith

The **Great Commandment** is found in **Deuteronomy 6:5** and **Leviticus 19:18**. This short statement contains the whole law of God. It sums up the Ten Commandments and emphasizes that love of God and neighbor are what God expects of his people. If the Great Commandment is kept, then Israel will grow and prosper and be happy as God's special people forever.

Working with the Text

• Read the text aloud. Use *The Language of Faith* to deepen the children's understanding of the highlighted term.
Why is it important to look at our lives in a prayerful way before we celebrate Reconciliation?
(We need to measure our actions against the Ten Commandments, the Beatitudes, the life of Jesus, and the teachings of the Church.)
Who helps us know the wrong choices we have made?
(the Holy Spirit)
Point out to the children that the Holy Spirit will also help us see the good choices we have made.

Working with the Pictures

• Draw attention to the large photograph in the center of the two pages. Invite volunteers to describe what they see.

• Help the children recognize the place as a small chapel inside a larger church. The large structure in the center is a *tabernacle*, the special container where consecrated Hosts are kept. Jesus is present in the tabernacle in a special way.
Why do you think the children are praying? (They are preparing to celebrate Reconciliation by examining their consciences. They are asking the Holy Spirit's help.)

How Do We Measure Up?

We know that we do not always live as God wants us to live. We do not always honor the commandments.

When we celebrate the Sacrament of Reconciliation, we look at our lives. We ask the Holy Spirit to help us see where we have made wrong choices.

This prayerful way of looking at our lives is called an **examination of conscience.** We measure our actions against the Ten Commandments, the Beatitudes, the life of Jesus, and the teachings of the Church.

34 : We Celebrate

Resource Center

The Language of Faith

An **examination of conscience** is a prayerful way of looking back on both our loving and unloving choices. When we examine our conscience, we remember God's love for us and how well we have responded to God's love. We recall, with the help of the Holy Spirit, those times when we did not act as we should and broke our promise to live according to God's law.

Link to Liturgy

Remind the children that at Mass there is a special time to pause and recall those ways in which we have broken our promise to live God's law and to ask forgiveness. We call this part of the Mass the *penitential rite.* This part of the Mass can take various forms and include various prayers, but it always reminds us that God is merciful.

We ask ourselves if we are really happy. We ask, "What would Jesus do?" Are we really living as God wants us to live? Have we failed to show love for God and for others? Have we been selfish or hurtful?

The Holy Spirit will not just help us see where we have gone wrong. God's loving Spirit will also show us how we can do better.

We Celebrate : 35

We Ask

What is conscience?

Conscience is the gift God gives us. Conscience is the judgment of our minds and hearts about whether our actions are good or evil. Conscience must be taught, or **formed**, to know the difference between right and wrong. *(Catechism, #1777, 1783)*

Working with the Text

Read the text aloud. Emphasize that the Holy Spirit also helps us know how we can do better.
What is one question we might ask ourselves as we examine our conscience? (Possible answers: What would Jesus do? Am I really living as God wants me to live? Have I been selfish or hurtful?)

Working with the Pictures

• Ask the children to look at the small photograph on this page. Invite volunteers to suggest what the girl in the picture might be doing. (Possible answer: reading the Bible.)

• Help the children recognize that God's word in the Bible, especially in the New Testament, can help us measure our actions to those of Jesus. God's word can also remind us of God's law, which God promises will make us truly happy if we live it out in our lives.

We Ask Invite a volunteer to read the question aloud. Then read the answer to the children, pausing frequently to see that they understand each sentence. Use *The Language of Faith* to help clarify the meaning of the bold-faced words. Remind the children to share this question and answer with their family members and prayer partners.

The Language of Faith

• Our ***conscience*** is the ongoing conversation that God has with us, pointing out to us when we have loved well and when we have not. When we listen to this conversation taking place within our hearts, we hear God's gentle voice calling us to come back to our promise to live the Great Commandment.

• Our conscience doesn't just happen; it is ***formed***. Our conscience begins to be formed in childhood with the teachings and example of our families and other important adults. We continue to learn more about God's laws and the teachings of the Church throughout our lives. All of this learning helps form, or mold, our conscience into an ability to choose right from wrong.

Enrichment

Make a WWJD reminder The girl in the small photo on this page is wearing a bracelet with the letters *WWJD*. These initials stand for *What Would Jesus Do?* Many people wear or carry something with these initials on it as a reminder to make good choices. Provide the children with a variety of art materials, and have them make their own *WWJD* bracelets, buttons, bookmarks, wallet cards, or stickers.

3. Close

Working with the Page

- Read the directions aloud. Allow the children time to think about what they will write or draw in each part of the prayer.

- Provide writing and drawing materials, and have the children complete the prayer. Play quiet music to accompany the children's work. This page may also be assigned as a take-home activity.

- Encourage the children to share their completed work now or during a later session.

Living Reconciliation at Home

Suggest these follow-up activities.

- With your family, make a list of general questions that each family member could ask himself or herself before celebrating Reconciliation.

- Take a few minutes each night before bedtime to think about the loving and unloving choices you made that day. Ask God's loving Spirit to help you make better choices tomorrow.

Living Reconciliation in the Parish

Have the children complete these activities in class or at home with family members or prayer partners.

- Review the examination of conscience on page 10 of *My Reconciliation Book*.

- Read and think about *Our Moral Guide* on pages 56–58. Talk about how the Beatitudes, the Ten Commandments, the Precepts of the Church, and the Works of Mercy can be guides for examining your conscience.

Getting Ready for Reconciliation

Have the children work in small groups to discuss this question.

If God hadn't given us the gift of a conscience, how might our lives be unhappy and hurtful?

Signs of Love

Finish the prayer by writing or drawing in each space.

Dear God, I love you. I will show my love for you by . . .

I love others, too. I will show my love for others by . . .

36 : We Live Reconciliation

Resource Center

Link to the Family

Distribute the Chapter 4 *Sharing Page* to be taken home. Encourage the children to take their books and Reconciliation booklets home to share with family members.

Link to Liturgy

Page 5 of *My Reconciliation Book* describes how an examination of conscience is incorporated into the communal celebration of the Sacrament of Reconciliation. Page 12 of *My Reconciliation Book* offers a sample examination of conscience for use in preparing for the individual celebration of the sacrament.

Send Us Your Spirit

The Holy Spirit helps us do what is right.

God our Father,
you made the human family
to live with you forever.

> **Send us your Holy Spirit!**
> **Open our hearts to your love!**

Open our ears to your voice
so that we may turn to you
with sorrow for our sins.

> **Send us your Holy Spirit!**
> **Open our hearts to your love!**

Help us grow in your love and grace,
which bring us true happiness,
so that we may live with you forever.

> **Send us your Holy Spirit!**
> **Open our hearts to your love!**

—*adapted from the Rite of Penance*

We Live Reconciliation : 37

Working with the Page

- Spend a few moments looking back through this chapter with the children. Ask volunteers to comment on their favorite parts of the Scripture story, favorite pictures, or new things they learned.

- Direct the children's attention to the symbols that make up the page border. Invite volunteers to describe the connection between these symbols and the chapter theme. (The tablets of the law and the hearts remind us to examine our consciences in light of the commandments. The doves are signs of the Holy Spirit, who helps us examine our consciences.)

- Have the children bring their books to the classroom prayer space or the church. Gather around a table or in the Eucharistic chapel or Reconciliation room. If possible, have the children's families and their prayer partners join you for the prayer.

Prayer Teach the children the response to the prayer on this page: "Send us your Holy Spirit! Open our hearts to your love!" Lead the children in the prayer, beginning and ending with the Sign of the Cross. See *Music for Prayer* for suggested songs to accompany this closing prayer.

Music for Prayer

Some songs that might accompany this closing prayer are "Come, O Holy Spirit," "Change Our Hearts," "Spirit, Come," or a song from the *Celebrating Our Faith* CD.

Enrichment

You may wish to precede the prayer with an examination of conscience. Use the examination of conscience on page 59 as a model. Pause for a few seconds after each question to allow the children to reflect silently.

Notes

WE ASK FORGIVENESS

Key Content Summary

Accepting God's forgiveness for sin means taking responsibility for our actions and making a decision to change. Confession of sin to the priest, who acts in the place of Jesus, is the way we acknowledge our responsibility. Accepting and doing a penance is a sign that we are willing, with God's help, to make things right.

Planning the Chapter

Open	Pacing Guide *Suggested time/Your time*	Content	Objectives	Materials
	10–20 min./ ___ min.	**We Are Invited,** pp. 38–39	• Recognize the importance of accepting responsibility for our actions and promising to do better.	• music for prayer (optional)

Build				
	35–45 min./ ___ min.	**We Remember,** pp. 40–41	• Recall the story of Zacchaeus, a sinner who changed his life.	• copies of script on pages HA9–HA10, simple props and costumes (optional)
		We Celebrate, pp. 42–43	• Identify the importance of doing penance. • Describe confession and accepting a penance in the Sacrament of Reconciliation.	

Close				
	15 min./ ___ min.	**We Live Reconciliation,** pp. 44–45	• Celebrate God's love.	• writing and drawing materials • *My Reconciliation Book* • Chapter 5 *Sharing Page* • music for prayer (optional)

Catechism Background

See Catechism of the Catholic Church, #1455–1456, 1467.

Doctrinal Foundation The therapeutic benefits of private confession were recognized by the founders of modern psychoanalysis, who based the analytic process on this ancient ritual. "Confession is good for the soul," the proverb says, and the benefits are far greater than the mere relief we feel when we let go of a painful secret. In the Church's history, private confession grew out of the Celtic monks' practice of sharing one's spiritual progress (or lack of it) with an *anam-cara*, a "soul friend," or spiritual director. Even though we celebrate the Sacrament of Reconciliation in a communal way today, the confession of sin, acceptance of a penance, and absolution are still celebrated privately, except in cases of emergency. This underlines the importance of personal accountability for sin and its consequences and allows the confessor to tailor the penance to be most helpful to the penitent's circumstances. "If you have sinned, you should tell each other what you have done. Then you can pray for one another and be healed" *(James 5:16)*.

One-Minute Retreat

Read

"The confession of evil works is the first beginning of good works."

—*Saint Augustine*

Reflect

When have I experienced the benefits of confession?

How can I use confession and the receiving of a penance to help my growth in faith?

Pray

Jesus, soul-friend,
help me and the children see you
in the priest who hears our confessions.
May we be open to your loving direction
in the penances we receive.
Give us the courage
to accept responsibility for our wrong choices
and the grace to make better ones.
Amen.

Library Links

Books for Children

Jesus and the Grumpy Little Man, by Carol Greene (Concordia Press).

The Story of Zacchaeus, by Marty Rhodes Figley (B. Eerdmans).

Two retellings of the story of Zacchaeus for children.

Books for Adults

Confession Can Change Your Life, by David Knight (St. Anthony Messenger Press).

The effects of conversion on everyday living.

"How to Go to Confession," by Leonard Foley OFM (*Catholic Update;* St. Anthony Messenger Press).

Why Confess Your Sins to a Priest? by Rev. John Dowling (Liguori).

The role of the priest as minister of the Sacrament of Reconciliation.

Why Go to Confession? Questions and Answers About Sacramental Reconciliation, by Rev. Joseph M. Champlin (St. Anthony Messenger Press).

A guide to the Rite of Penance.

Multimedia for Children

Celebrating Our Faith (CD) (produced by GIA; BROWN-ROA).

One or more songs from this collection may be used to enhance classroom prayer and liturgy.

Celebrating Reconciliation with Children (6-part video series) (produced by Salt River Production Group; BROWN-ROA).

Segment 5: We Ask Forgiveness is designed for use with this chapter.

A Child's First Penance (video) (Liguori).

The video reviews the steps in the Rite of Penance.

Multimedia for Adults

The God Who Reconciles (video) (Franciscan Communications/St. Anthony Messenger Press).

This video uses story, witness, teaching, and song to explore the meaning of the Sacrament of Reconciliation.

WE ARE INVITED

1. Open

Gathering Invite the children to think of a story, movie, or TV program in which one of the characters did something on purpose that hurt someone else. Invite volunteers to share their examples.

Prayer Pray the opening prayer with the children. See *Music for Prayer* for suggested songs to accompany the opening prayer.

Working with the Text

• Read aloud the opening question on this page. Pause to allow the children to respond silently.

• Continue reading aloud the text on this page. Pause to allow the children time to reflect on it.
What makes a mistake a mistake?
(We don't make mistakes on purpose.)
What makes a sin a sin?
(We sin when we make a wrong choice on purpose.)

Working with the Pictures

Draw attention to the photograph of the two boys and their mother. Invite volunteers to describe what they think might have happened. (Possible answers: The boys had a fight over a toy; one boy broke his brother's toy.)
What do you think the mother is telling her son? (Possible answer: that he made a wrong choice and should fix the toy.)

WE ASK FORGIVENESS

Dear God—Father, Son, and Holy Spirit— you call us to make peace when we do wrong. Help us ask forgiveness and do penance. Amen!

Have you ever done something that hurt someone else?

Everyone makes mistakes. Everyone makes wrong choices at some time. When you choose to do something you know is wrong, you sin. Sin is not the same thing as making a mistake.

38 : We Are Invited

Resource Center

Music for Prayer

Some suggestions for music to enhance this prayer are "Hold Us in Your Mercy," "Nada Te Turbe (Nothing Can Trouble)," or "Kyrie" from the *Celebrating Our Faith* CD.

Teaching Tip

Clarifying concepts Some children may have a difficult time distinguishing among mistakes, accidents, and sins. Provide the class with several age-appropriate examples of each. Discuss each example with the children, asking them to suggest why the action was or was not sinful, that is, deliberately wrong or hurtful.

Notes

Sin hurts. It hurts you. It hurts others. Part of healing the hurt is taking **responsibility** for your actions. You admit that you did wrong. Then you do something with God's help to make things right.

The Sacrament of Reconciliation gives us a way to admit that we have done wrong. We **confess** our sins. And the sacrament gives us a way to make things right with God's help. We are given a **penance** to do. Accepting and doing our penance is a sign that we want to grow more loving.

We Are Invited : 39

Working with the Text

• Read aloud the text on this page, or summarize it in your own words.

• Use *The Language of Faith* to help clarify the meanings of the bold-faced words.

• Pause to allow the children to reflect on the text.
  Why is it important to take responsibility for our actions? (By taking responsibility, we can then do something to make things right again.)
  Which sacrament gives us a way to make things right again with God's help? (the Sacrament of Reconciliation)
  What does accepting and doing a penance for our sins help us do? (grow more loving)

The Language of Faith

• To take *responsibility* for our words and actions means to accept the praise or the blame for what we have done. A sign of maturity is being responsible for both the good things and the wrong things we have done.

• To *confess* our sins means to tell them aloud to the priest. The practice of individual confession grew out of Irish monastic custom.

• A *penance* given to us by the priest in the Sacrament of Reconciliation is a prayer or an action that will help us make things right. Doing a penance shows God that we are sorry for our sins and want to do better.

Teaching Tip

Children of this age may still find it difficult to accept responsibility for their wrong actions. It is common for them to want to place the blame on others and thus avoid the consequences of their behavior. Growing in moral responsibility is a lifelong process. Praise the children whenever you witness them accepting responsibility, and be patient with them during those times when they fail to do so. Part of their moral growth is learning how to accept themselves with all their imperfections. Through your unconditional acceptance of them, they will come to know the infinite love and acceptance of God.

2. Build

Working with the Text

- Invite the children to choose comfortable positions for sharing the Scripture story.
- Write the name *Zacchaeus* on the board. Invite volunteers to tell what they already know about this person who had a special meeting with Jesus.
- Read aloud or retell the story on this page.
- Help the children discuss the part of the story that is on this page.
  Why was Zacchaeus not popular with the people of his town? (He cheated people on their taxes. He charged too much money and kept the extra money for himself.)
  Why did Zacchaeus want to see Jesus? (He had heard that Jesus healed people and forgave sins.)
  What did Zacchaeus do so that he could get a glimpse of Jesus as Jesus walked by? (He climbed a tree.)

Working with the Pictures

Draw attention to the illustration on these pages. Invite volunteers to describe what they see.
  Why do you think Zaccaheus is pointing to himself? (He can't believe that Jesus is inviting himself to *his* house for lunch.)
  Why are the people grumbling? (They don't eat with sinners, and they don't think Jesus should either.)

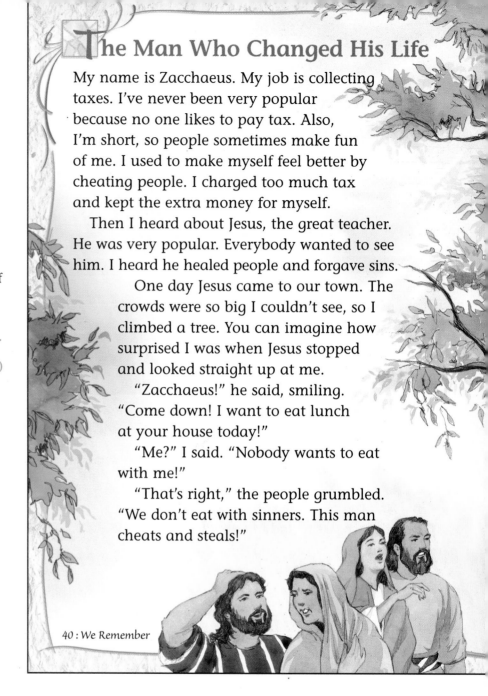

The Man Who Changed His Life

My name is Zacchaeus. My job is collecting taxes. I've never been very popular because no one likes to pay tax. Also, I'm short, so people sometimes make fun of me. I used to make myself feel better by cheating people. I charged too much tax and kept the extra money for myself.

Then I heard about Jesus, the great teacher. He was very popular. Everybody wanted to see him. I heard he healed people and forgave sins.

One day Jesus came to our town. The crowds were so big I couldn't see, so I climbed a tree. You can imagine how surprised I was when Jesus stopped and looked straight up at me.

"Zacchaeus!" he said, smiling. "Come down! I want to eat lunch at your house today!"

"Me?" I said. "Nobody wants to eat with me!"

"That's right," the people grumbled. "We don't eat with sinners. This man cheats and steals!"

40 : We Remember

Resource Center

Scripture Background

This amusing story of conversion and forgiveness, restitution and healing, is found only in the **Gospel of Luke**. Zacchaeus, a chief tax collector, was despised for his collaboration with the Romans, which made him unclean by religious standards. Not only did this man collect taxes for the Romans, but he also overcharged the people, to make himself wealthy. It would not have been a Jewish custom to share a meal with such a public sinner. Jesus surprised the people by going to Zacchaeus's home and sharing a meal.

Art Background

The illustration on these pages depicting Zacchaeus up in a tree is a favorite image from this story of forgiveness for Christians of all ages. Responsible Christians recognize themselves in Zacchaeus. They seek healing and reconciliation. The story is also a timeless lesson to the Christian community, reminding it that its task is to break down the barriers that keep others at arm's length, despite the best religious reasons.

But Jesus just held out his hand. I nearly fell out of the tree. I led Jesus straight to my house. I fed him and his friends a big lunch. And then before I knew it, I was crying.

"I'm sorry," I told Jesus. "Those people were right. I am a sinner. I did cheat. I did steal. But I want to change my life. From this day on, with God's help, I will never cheat or steal. And I will give back four times the amount to everyone I've ever cheated."

Jesus gave me a hug. "Today," Jesus said, "God's forgiveness has come to this house!"

—based on Luke 19:1–10

We Remember : 41

Working with the Text

- Continue reading aloud or retelling the Scripture story on this page.
- Help the children discuss the text. **Why did Zacchaeus feel sad after serving lunch to Jesus and his friends?** (Zacchaeus was starting to feel bad about the way he had treated the people.)
Feeling bad about what he had done made Zacchaeus want to do something. What was it? (He told Jesus he was sorry and that he wanted to change his life.)
How would Zacchaeus show that he really was sorry and wanted to change his life? (by offering to give back four times the amount he stole from the people)
What did Jesus say and do to show Zacchaeus that he believed him? (Jesus hugged Zacchaeus and told him that God's forgiveness had been given to him.)
How do you think Zacchaeus treated people after that? (Possible answer: He treated them with respect and did not cheat them.)

Link to Liturgy

Tell the children that the story of Zacchaeus is sometimes read at Sunday Mass. It is a story taken from the **Gospel of Luke** and so is read aloud by the presiding priest or the deacon. The part of the Mass when we listen to God's word from the Gospels and from the other books of the Bible is called the *Liturgy of the Word*. Help the children recall the gospel reading proclaimed at last Sunday's liturgy. Encourage them to listen for the gospel reading each time they gather for Mass.

Enrichment

Role-play the Scripture story Use or adapt the script on pages HA9–HA10 to have the children act out the story of Zacchaeus. Suggestions for simple costumes and props can be found on page HA8.

Working with the Text

- Read aloud the text on this page.
- Use the following questions to help the children understand what takes place during the Rite of Penance.
  To whom do we confess our sins? (the priest)
  In whose name does the priest act? (in Jesus' name)
  After we have confessed our sins, what does the priest help us do? (He helps us find ways to make things right.)
  What does the priest give us to help us make things right? (a penance)
- Help the children connect the penance given by the priest with the sin or sins being confessed. Remind them that a penance helps us show that we are sorry and want to do better.

Working with the Pictures

Direct attention to the photograph of the boy talking with the priest at a communal celebration of the Sacrament of Reconciliation. Invite volunteers to describe what they see in the picture.

Confession and Penance

Zacchaeus confessed his sins to Jesus. Then he promised to return four times the amount of money he had stolen.

In the Sacrament of Reconciliation, we do what Zacchaeus did. We confess our sins to the priest, who acts in the name of Jesus. We talk with the priest about how we can make things right.

The priest gives us a penance to do. The penance may be to spend some time praying. Or it may be an action connected to the sin, such as returning stolen property or helping repair something broken.

42 : We Celebrate

Resource Center

Teaching Tip

Providing practice It is normal to be nervous about doing something for the first time. To help the children feel more comfortable about celebrating this sacrament, take time to role-play the Rite of Penance with them. Invite volunteers to act as penitents, giving them or having the class give them a common "sin" of second graders to confess. Take the part of the priest. Role-play the confessing of sins and the accepting of the penance. Be sure the penance you give is related to the sin confessed. Make the child feel as comfortable as possible, allowing for nervous laughter and conversation. Invite other volunteers to role-play with you, if time permits.

Link to Liturgy

- Explain to the children that because there are many people wishing to confess their sins and accept a penance at a communal service, there are usually several priests available. The priests often sit at different places in the church. The boy and the priest in the picture above are sitting in a place in the church where no one else can overhear their conversation.

- Explain that this part of the celebration is always private between the priest, who is acting in the place of Jesus, and the person who is confessing.

Doing penance helps us take responsibility for our actions. It reminds us to think twice about how our choices might hurt others. Penance is not punishment. It is a way to learn and grow more loving. Penance is so important that our celebration of the Sacrament of Reconciliation is called the **Rite of Penance**.

Whether we celebrate Reconciliation individually or communally, confession and the giving of a penance almost always take place privately between the penitent and the priest.

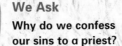

We Celebrate : 43

We Ask

Why do we confess our sins to a priest?

Confessing our sins aloud helps us take responsibility for our actions. Only God forgives sin, but the priest acts as God's minister by listening to our confession, giving us a penance, and encouraging us to avoid sin in the future. The priest may never tell anyone what he hears in confession. *(Catechism, #1455–1456, 1467)*

WE CELEBRATE
Build *Continued*
Working with the Text

• Read aloud the text on this page. Use *The Language of Faith* to help clarify the meaning of the *Rite of Penance*.

• Stress that the penance we accept from the priest is not punishment. It is a way to help us grow in God's love.

• Briefly explain the differences between individual and communal celebrations of Reconciliation. Refer to pages 60 and 61 in the child's book. Tell the children that the same important parts of the rite are present in both.

Working with the Pictures

Ask the children to look at the photograph on this page. Point out to the children the stole worn around the priest's neck. Tell them that the priest's stole is a sign that he is acting in the name of Jesus.

We Ask Invite a volunteer to read the question aloud. Then read the answer to the children, pausing to see if they understand each part of the answer. Reinforce the idea that only God can forgive sins. Remind the children to share this question and the answer with their family members and prayer partners.

The Language of Faith

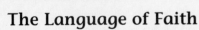

The **Rite of Penance** is the official name for the Sacrament of Reconciliation. The sacrament took this name because of the importance of accepting and carrying out the penance given by the priest. By doing the penance, the penitent is showing his or her willingness to stop the wrongful action and change his or her life. Penance is not the only important part of the sacrament. Asking forgiveness, accepting God's mercy, and being reconciled are all important to the celebration of the sacrament.

3. Close

Working with the Page

- Read the directions aloud. Allow the children time to think about what they will write or draw on each side of the vase.

- Provide writing and drawing materials, and have the children complete the activity. Play quiet music to accompany the children's work and to sustain a prayerful atmosphere. This page may also be assigned as a take-home activity.

- Encourage the children to share their completed work now or during a later session.

Living Reconciliation at Home

Suggest these follow-up activities.

- With your family, have a prayer celebration that celebrates God's forgiveness.

- Write a thank-you note to God, telling God that you are grateful for the opportunity to celebrate Reconciliation for the first time.

Living Reconciliation in the Parish

Have the children complete these activities in class or at home with family members or prayer partners.

- Color pages 6, 7, and 13 of *My Reconciliation Book*.

- With a partner, practice confessing sins and accepting a penance. (Do not confess actual sins. Use examples of wrong choices someone your age might make.)

Getting Ready for Reconciliation

Have the children work in small groups to discuss this question.

What is there to celebrate about the Sacrament of Reconciliation?

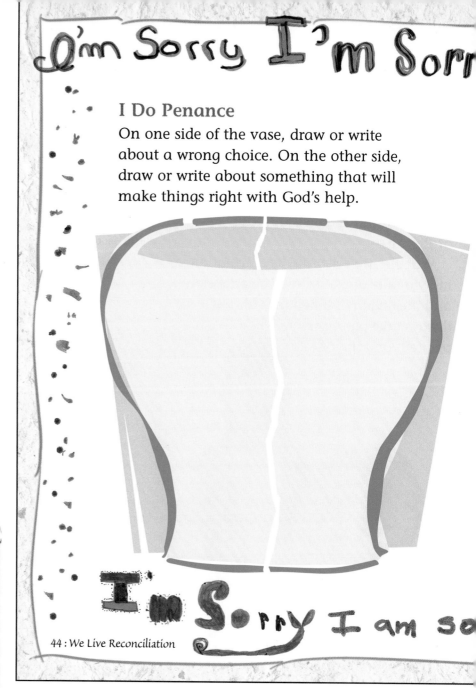

I Do Penance

On one side of the vase, draw or write about a wrong choice. On the other side, draw or write about something that will make things right with God's help.

44 : We Live Reconciliation

Resource Center

Link to the Family

Distribute the Chapter 5 *Sharing Page* to be taken home. Encourage the children to take their books and Reconciliation booklets home to share with family members.

Link to Liturgy

Pages 6 and 7 of *My Reconciliation Book* cover the general confession of sins and individual confession and absolution during a communal celebration. Page 13 describes individual confession and the receiving of a penance. Review these pages with the children, familiarizing them with their role as the penitent in the sacramental celebration.

God Loves Us

We admit that we have done wrong. But we accept God's forgiveness when we show sorrow and promise to do better.

God our Father,
sometimes we have not behaved as your
children should.
But you love us and come to us.
We have quarreled.
We have been lazy.
But you love us and come to us.
We have not been helpful.
We have not done good to others
when we had the chance.
But you love us and come to us.
With Jesus our Brother
we come before you
and ask you to forgive our sins.
Amen!

—based on the Rite of Penance

We Live Reconciliation : 45

Working with the Page

• Spend a few moments looking back through this chapter with the children. Ask volunteers to comment on their favorite parts of the lesson or on new things they learned.

• Direct the children's attention to the symbols that make up the page border. Invite volunteers to describe the connection between the symbols and the chapter content. (The border is made up of the words "I'm sorry" in children's handwriting; sorrow for sin is the first step in taking responsibility, confessing, and accepting a penance.)

• Have the children bring their books to the classroom prayer space or the church. Gather around a table or in the Reconciliation room. If possible, have the children's families and their prayer partners join you for the prayer.

Prayer Teach the children the response to the prayer on this page: "But you love us and come to us." Lead the children in the prayer, beginning and ending with the Sign of the Cross. See *Music for Prayer* for suggested songs to accompany this closing prayer.

Music for Prayer

Songs that might accompany this closing prayer are "I Will Praise You, Lord," "Change Our Hearts," or "Amazing Grace." You may also wish to choose a song from the *Celebrating Our Faith* CD.

Notes

WE GO FORTH IN PARDON AND PEACE

Key Content Summary

In the Sacrament of Reconciliation, we celebrate God's forgiveness, asked for in our prayer of contrition and given to us through the ministry of the Church in absolution. Reconciliation restores us to a graced relationship with God, with the community, and with all creation.

Planning the Chapter

Open	Pacing Guide *Suggested time/Your time*	Content	Objectives	Materials
	10–20 min./ _____ **min.**	**We Are Invited,** pp. 46–47	• Recognize the connection between expressing sorrow and being forgiven.	• music for prayer (optional)

Build				
	35–45 min./ _____ **min.**	**We Remember,** pp. 48–49	• Recall Jesus' meeting with the woman whose sins were forgiven.	
		We Celebrate, pp. 50–51	• Identify the effects of sacramental absolution. • Describe the Act of Contrition and prayer of absolution in Reconciliation.	• index cards, art materials, religious images (optional)

Close				
	15 min./ _____ **min.**	**We Live Reconciliation,** pp. 52–53	• Celebrate God's gift of forgiving love.	• writing and drawing materials • *My Reconciliation Book* • Chapter 6 *Sharing Page* • copies of preparation certificates, p. HA11 • music for prayer (optional) • colored paper strips, writing materials, stapler (optional)

Catechism Background

See Catechism of the Catholic Church, #1469.

Doctrinal Foundation   The Sacrament of Reconciliation has the powerful effect of bringing back together that which has been separated or broken—the bond of graced relationship between each person and God, the human community, and all creation. The reference to creation may give us pause. We know that sin disrupts our relationship with God and with others. But why does the Church expressly teach that sacramental absolution reconciles us with creation? The disorder, the radical fracture that sin brings about in our lives, extends to all things because all things came from God's hand and share the same destiny. All creation is called to be returned, in grace, to the wholeness and beauty original sin disrupted. The final return will signal the coming of God's kingdom in fullness. Each time we participate in the Sacrament of Reconciliation, we experience a foretaste of the joy for which we, and all things, were created. "In fact, all creation is eagerly waiting for God to show who his children are. Meanwhile, creation is confused, but not because it wants to be confused. God made it this way in the hope that creation would be set free from decay and would share in the glorious freedom of his children" *(Romans 8:19–21).*

One-Minute Retreat

Read

"Being holy doesn't mean never falling into sin. It means being able to say, 'Yes, Lord, I have fallen a thousand times. But thanks to you I have got up again a thousand and one times.'"

—*Dom Helder Camara*

Reflect

What are the most important effects of Reconciliation for me?

How does the possibility of God's forgiveness influence my own growth in holiness?

Pray

Dear God
—forgiving Father, redeeming Son, sanctifying Spirit—
thank you for the Sacrament of Reconciliation
and your call to holiness.
Help me guide the children to trust in your mercy
and turn to you with confidence
as they grow in faith and love.
Amen.

Library Links

Books for Children
Jesus Forgives My Sins, by Mary Terese Donze ASC (Liguori).
   A child's book about sacramental absolution.

Books for Adults
The Forgiving Family: First Steps To Reconciliation, by Carol Luebering (St. Anthony Messenger Press).
   Living the grace of Reconciliation at home.

Your Sins Are Forgiven You: Rediscovering the Sacrament of Reconciliation, by George Maloney (Alba House).
   A reflection on the transforming power of Reconciliation.

Multimedia for Children
Celebrating Our Faith (CD) (produced by GIA; BROWN-ROA).
   One or more songs from this collection may be used to enhance classroom prayer and liturgy.

Celebrating Reconciliation with Children (6-part video series) (produced by Salt River Production Group; BROWN-ROA).
   Segment 6: We Go Forth in Pardon and Peace is designed for use with this chapter.

Skateboard (video) (Franciscan Communications/ St. Anthony Messenger Press).
   A parable of Reconciliation in the family.

Multimedia for Adults
Lord of Mercy: Reconciliation (video) (BROWN-ROA).
   A celebration of the Sacrament of Reconciliation.

WE ARE INVITED

1. Open

Gathering Ask the children to think of a time when someone told them that he or she was sorry. Invite volunteers to share how the person demonstrated or expressed his or her sorrow.

Prayer Pray the opening prayer together. See *Music for Prayer* for suggested songs to accompany the prayer.

Working with the Text

- Read aloud the text on this page. Invite the children to name other ways we can tell someone that we are sorry.

- Read the last sentence aloud, and invite volunteers to respond. Help the children understand that when we say we are sorry, we want the other person to tell us that we are forgiven.

Working with the Pictures

Draw attention to the photograph of the mother and daughter hugging. Invite volunteers to describe what they see.

How is the girl showing her mother that she is sorry?
(by giving her a hug)

What might the mother say?
(Possible answers: I forgive you; That's OK; I know you are sorry, and I love you.)

WE GO FORTH IN PARDON AND PEACE

Dear God—Father, Son, and Holy Spirit— you free us from sin when we are sorry. Help us grow in peace and love. Amen!

How do you show someone you are sorry?

You can use words. You can use gestures, like a hug or a handshake. Sometimes tears are a sign that you are sorry.

What do you want to happen when you say you are sorry?

46 : We Are Invited

Resource Center

Music for Prayer

Some suggestions for music to enhance this prayer are "Over My Head," "Dona Nobis Pacem (Grant Us Peace)," or "Joyfully Singing" from the *Celebrating Our Faith* CD.

Notes

In the Sacrament of Reconciliation, we show sorrow for sin by praying an **Act of Contrition**. In the prayer we tell God how sorry we are for having sinned. We promise to do better.

When we say we are sorry, we want our wrong choices to be forgiven. And we want the chance to start over.

In the Sacrament of Reconciliation, we celebrate God's forgiveness. In the name of God and the Church, the priest gives us **absolution**. We start fresh, with joy.

We Are Invited : 47

WE ARE INVITED
Open *Continued*

Working with the Text

- Read aloud the text on this page. Use *The Language of Faith* to clarify the meanings of the bold-faced terms.

- Invite the children to discuss the text. **How do we show sorrow for sin in the Sacrament of Reconciliation?** (by praying an Act of Contrition) **What do we call the words of forgiveness that the priest says in the name of God and the Church?** (absolution)

Working with the Pictures

Draw attention to the photograph on this page. Invite volunteers to suggest what they think is happening in the picture. Be sure the children understand that the priest's outstretched hand is a sign of the blessing of the Trinity. The priest is praying the prayer of absolution. **How do you think the boy is feeling as he hears the words of absolution?** (Possible answers: happy, filled with joy, forgiven, peaceful.)

The Language of Faith

- An **Act of Contrition** is a prayerful way of telling God we are sorry for the hurt we have caused and that we intend to do better. We can choose from many suggested texts for this prayer, or we may express contrition in our own words.

- **Absolution** is the forgiveness of sin and remittance of temporal punishment granted to us in the Sacrament of Reconciliation. The priest's prayer and gesture are the effective signs of God's forgiveness. The word *absolve* means "to wash away." We believe that the absolution we receive in the Sacrament of Reconciliation washes away all of our sins.

Working with the Text

- Invite the children to find comfortable positions for sharing the Scripture story.
- Read aloud the Scripture story on this page. Use an engaging tone of voice to help the children picture in their imaginations the action of the story.
- After reading the story, discuss it with the children.
  Why was everyone looking at the woman? (They knew she was a great sinner and had not been invited to the banquet.)
  Why did the woman come to the banquet? (She had to see Jesus because she wanted him to know that she was not a sinner anymore. She had been forgiven by God.)
  What did she do to show her sorrow? (She washed Jesus' feet with her tears, dried them with her hair, and poured expensive perfumed oil over them.)

Working with the Pictures

Ask the children to look at the illustration on this page. Help them identify the three people in the picture: Jesus, the forgiven woman, and Simon.
What do you expect Simon to say to this woman? (Possible answers: Stop doing that; Why have you come to my house uninvited? Leave him alone; You are a sinner; Go away!)

The Forgiven Woman

I knew everyone was looking at me. After all, I was known all over town as a terrible sinner. No one had invited me to this banquet at the house of Simon, a holy man.

But I had to see Jesus. I had to let him know that I wasn't a sinner anymore. I had been given the great gift of God's loving forgiveness.

I couldn't help it. As soon as I saw Jesus, I fell down before him. My tears washed the dust from his feet. My hair dried them. Then I poured sweet perfumed oil on his feet. The jar had cost me everything I had in the world, but it was worth it.

48 : We Remember

Resource Center

Scripture Background

Luke's unique version of a healing story found in all four Gospels depicts some of the Pharisees trying to test whether or not Jesus is a true prophet. If he is, then he will know that the woman is a great sinner and, according to Jewish law, he will not allow her to come near him. However, while Jesus does not do what Simon, a Pharisee, expects, he shows that he is a great prophet—and more. Jesus recognizes that the woman must have been forgiven much because her love toward him was great. And Jesus is able to read the heart of Simon, his host. It is the outpouring of love rather than the woman's sinfulness that Jesus focuses on.

Art Background

The illustration on these pages shows the scene at Simon's house, where Jesus is attending a banquet. The uninvited woman has washed Jesus' feet with her tears and is drying them with her hair. It was customary for the host to provide water for the guests to wash their feet. This was a sign of hospitality and friendship. The welcomed guests were also anointed on their heads with oil and greeted with a kiss. But Simon did not provide Jesus with any of these warm gestures. Instead, it was a woman considered by many to be a great sinner who provided Jesus with these customary gestures of love—and more—as she washed his feet.

"I know what you're thinking, Simon," Jesus said to his shocked host. "How can I let this great sinner anywhere near me? But I can tell by her tears and her love that she has been forgiven."

"Yes, but . . ." Simon sputtered.

"Think of it this way," Jesus said. "What if two people owe you money—one a lot and one a little. You tell both of them they don't have to pay. Which one is going to be more grateful?"

Simon began to understand. "The person who has been forgiven more will be happier," he said.

"This woman has done more for me than you did," Jesus said. "That's how I know how much she has been forgiven."

Jesus looked at me with kindness. "Your sins are forgiven," he said. "Now go in peace." As I walked out of Simon's great hall with everyone's eyes on me, I held my head up. I felt like dancing.

—based on Luke 7:36–50

We Remember : 49

Working with the Pictures

Direct attention to the part of the large illustration on this page. Invite volunteers to suggest who these people might be.

What do you think the woman is carrying on her head?
(Help the children recognize that it is a large bowl of food to be served at the banquet. This was, and still is, a common way of carrying heavy items in some parts of the world.)

Working with the Text

• Continue reading the Scripture story.

• Help the children discuss the story by asking these questions.

Why was Simon upset by how Jesus was treating the woman?
(He didn't think it was right for a sinful woman to be near Jesus.)

What did Jesus say about the woman? (that she had been forgiven for many sins and that she was grateful)

What did Jesus say to the woman? ("Your sins are forgiven. Now go in peace.")

How did Jesus' words and actions make the woman feel?
(Possible answers: at peace, full of joy, loved.)

Link to Liturgy

Sometimes the Mass, the celebration of the Eucharist, is described as a banquet. A banquet is much more than a meal. It is an elaborate feast given either in honor of someone or to mark some great accomplishment. The Mass is an elaborate feast at which we are fed with the word of God and with the Body and Blood of Christ. It is God our Father whom we honor at this great feast because of the many gifts he has bestowed on us, especially the great gift of Jesus. The celebration of the Eucharist is also described as a foretaste of the heavenly banquet in which we will all share one day in heaven.

Working with the Text

- Read aloud or summarize the text on this page. Use *The Language of Faith* to clarify the meaning of the word *litany*.

- Explain to the children that any prayer of contrition, or sorrow, is acceptable in the Sacrament of Reconciliation. We can also use our own words in a prayer of contrition. **Why do you think it is necessary for us to pray a prayer of sorrow in the Sacrament of Reconciliation?** (It shows that we are sorry, we want God's forgiveness, and we promise to do better.)

- Remind the children that at a communal celebration of the sacrament, the parish community is present. By praying together a litany of sorrow, everyone present is admitting having sinned, showing sorrow, asking God's forgiveness, and promising to do better.

Working with the Pictures

Draw attention to the photograph on this page. Invite volunteers to describe what they see. **What kind of prayer may be on the back of the holy card the boy is holding in the picture?** (an Act of Contrition) **What do you see on the front of the holy card?** (a picture of Jesus comforting someone who is sorry for having sinned)

Contrition and Absolution

Contrition, or sorrow for sin, is necessary for accepting God's forgiveness. In the Sacrament of Reconciliation, we show contrition in the words of a prayer. There are many versions of the Act of Contrition, but each one says the same thing. We have sinned. We are sorry. We ask God's forgiveness. We promise to do better.

In a communal celebration of the sacrament, our prayer of contrition is followed by a **litany** spoken by the whole group. The Lord's Prayer always concludes the litany. In individual celebrations, the penitent prays an Act of Contrition after confessing and receiving a penance.

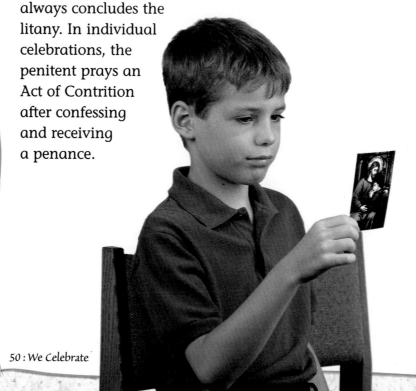

50 : We Celebrate

Resource Center

The Language of Faith

A **litany** is a form of prayer in which short petitions or intercessions are interspersed with a refrain. This type of prayer originated in the liturgies of the Eastern Rites, which still maintain numerous litanies. The *Kyrie* at Mass is an example of a litany that originated in the East. The general intercessions of the Mass are also prayed in the form of a litany.

Enrichment

Make a prayer card Provide blank index cards and art supplies (including images from holy cards and recycled Christmas cards if you wish), and have the children make their own prayer cards containing an Act of Contrition. The children may decorate the reverse side of the card with cutout or drawn religious pictures or symbols of forgiveness. See page 55 for prayer texts.

The Sacrament of Reconciliation almost always includes private absolution of the penitent by the priest. Holding out his hand as a sign of the Holy Spirit's blessing, the priest prays, "Through the ministry of the Church, may God give you **pardon** and peace, and I absolve you from your sins in the name of the Father, and of the Son, and of the Holy Spirit." We answer, "Amen."

Our celebration almost always ends with a joyful song or prayer of thanks to God. Like the woman whom Jesus forgave, we are overflowing with gratitude for God's love and mercy. We go forth in peace.

What does the Sacrament of Reconciliation do for us?

The Sacrament of Reconciliation does exactly what its name describes. Through sacramental confession and absolution, we are **reconciled**, or brought back together, with God. That reconciliation has other effects. We are reconciled with our own conscience, allowing us to feel inner peace. We are reconciled with others, especially those whom we have hurt. We are reconciled with the Christian community, making the whole Church stronger. And we are reconciled with all God's creation. *(Catechism, #1469)*

We Celebrate : 51

WE CELEBRATE
Build *Continued*

Working with the Text

• Read aloud or summarize the text on this page. Use *The Language of Faith* to clarify the meaning of the word *pardon*.

• Invite the children to reflect on and discuss the text.
What does the priest ask for us in the prayer of absolution? (pardon and peace)
What are we absolved from? (our sins)
In whose name are we absolved? (in the name of the Father, and of the Son, and of the Holy Spirit)

Working with the Pictures

Direct attention to the photograph at the bottom of this page.
Why do you think this group of children and the adult are singing? (They have just celebrated the Sacrament of Reconciliation and are singing a joyful song. They are filled with gratitude for God's love and mercy.)

We Ask Invite a volunteer to read the question aloud. Then read the answer to the children, pausing to see that they understand each sentence. Use *The Language of Faith* to help children review what it means to be *reconciled*. Remind the children to share this question and answer with their family members and prayer partners.

The Language of Faith

• The term **pardon** means "forgiveness" or "release from punishment." The children may be familiar with secular uses of this word, such as saying "pardon me" when interrupting or disturbing someone, or a criminal offender's receiving a pardon (release from sentence) from a higher court or the governor.

• Remind the children that to be **reconciled** means to be brought back together in peace. The same word that gives its name to the Sacrament of Reconciliation is also commonly used to describe the reunion of separated family members or the building of peace between nations.

Catechetical Background

The Sacrament of Reconciliation involves many concepts that are not within the grasp of young children. When teaching the different parts of the rite, always emphasize God's abundant love, mercy, and forgiveness for each of us, no matter how terrible our sin. Discourage any ideas that God is always trying to catch us in a sin or that God no longer loves us when we sin. Teaching by word and example that God is a God of love who keeps his promises to us, no matter what, will create in the children a healthy attitude toward sin, forgiveness, and the Sacrament of Reconciliation.

3. Close

Working with the Page

- Read the directions aloud. Allow the children time to think about what they will write for the prayer activity.
- Provide writing and drawing materials, and have the children write the prayer. Play quiet music as the children work. This page may also be assigned as a take-home activity.
- Encourage the children to share their completed work now or during the closing prayer celebration.

Living Reconciliation at Home

Suggest these follow-up activities.

- Discuss as a family what it means to be sorry for making a wrong choice.
- Pray your own Act of Contrition, or any prayer of sorrow, each night before going to bed.

Living Reconciliation in the Parish

Have the children complete these activities in class or at home with family members or prayer partners.

- Color pages 6–9 and 14–16 of *My Reconciliation Book*.
- Learn an Act of Contrition and the prayers and responses associated with the Concluding Rite of the Sacrament of Reconciliation.

Getting Ready for First Reconciliation

Have the children work in small groups to discuss this question.

How will the Sacrament of Reconciliation improve your friendships with God and your family members and friends?

I Promise to Do Better

On the lines, write your own Act of Contrition. Then decorate the frame with joyful colors.

Resource Center

Link to the Family

Distribute the Chapter 6 *Sharing Page* to be taken home. Encourage the children to take their books and Reconciliation booklets home to share with family members and save as keepsakes.

Link to Liturgy

Pages 6–9 and 14–16 of *My Reconciliation Book* cover the prayers and actions associated with the Act of Contrition, absolution, and the Concluding Rite of the Sacrament of Reconciliation. Go over these pages with the children, helping them become familiar with the prayers and responses. See page 55 of the child's book for prayers that may be used as an Act of Contrition.

Thank You, God!

We thank God for the Sacrament of Reconciliation.

God and Father of us all,
you have forgiven our sins.

Thank you for your mercy!

You have given us your peace.

Thank you for your peace!

Help us forgive one another.

Help us show mercy.

Help us work together for peace in the world.

Help us share peace.

Amen!

—based on the Rite of Penance

We Live Reconciliation : 53

Working with the Page

- Spend a few moments looking back over this chapter with the children. Invite volunteers to share their favorite parts of the lesson.

- Direct the children's attention to the symbols that make up the page border. Invite volunteers to describe the connection between these symbols and the chapter theme. **(The broken chain is a sign of the release from sin that comes with absolution. The butterfly, which emerges from the cocoon, is a sign of the new life we celebrate in the Sacrament of Reconciliation.)**

- Have the children bring their books to the classroom space or the church. Gather around a table or in the Eucharistic chapel or main sanctuary. If possible, have the children's families and their prayer partners join you for the prayer.

- You may wish to copy and complete for each child the First Reconciliation preparation certificate on page HA11. Distribute completed certificates to the children at the concluding prayer service.

Prayer Teach the children the responses to the prayer on this page: *Thank you for your mercy! Thank you for your peace! Help us show mercy. Help us share peace.* Lead the children in the prayer, beginning and ending with the Sign of the Cross. See *Music for Prayer* for suggested songs to accompany this closing prayer.

Music for Prayer

If the children are learning a song of thanksgiving for their First Reconciliation celebration, have them sing it as part of the closing prayer. You may also wish to choose a song from the *Celebrating Our Faith* CD.

Enrichment

Make and break a chain Give each child a 1″ × 5″ length of colored paper. Have each child write on the paper a bad habit he or she would like to break, such as quarreling with family members or being lazy. (Remind the children **not** to put their names on the papers.) Gather the lengths of colored paper, and staple them, the written side facing in, into the links of a chain. Have the children line up as if for tug-of-war and, as a sign of the intention to do better, tug on the paper chain until the links break.

Notes

Catholic Prayers

These pages contain the texts of several traditional Catholic prayers. Refer the children to this section when you want to reinforce their familiarity with these prayers. Incorporate these prayers into the opening and closing prayers for each chapter.

The Sign of the Cross

Always begin and end classroom prayer with the Sign of the Cross. If necessary, model for the children the traditional gesture of signing oneself with the cross.

The Lord's Prayer

- Have the children suggest simple gestures to accompany the phrases of the prayer.
- Remind the children to listen for the Lord's Prayer at Mass and at communal Reconciliation services and to join in praying it.

The Hail Mary

- Play for the children a simple musical setting of the Hail Mary.
- Tell the children that this prayer to the mother of Jesus is part of many Catholic popular devotions.

Glory to the Father (Doxology)

Explain to the children that the word *doxology* means "words of praise."

Catholic Prayers

The Sign of the Cross

In the name of the Father,
and of the Son,
and of the Holy Spirit.
Amen.

The Lord's Prayer

Our Father, who art in heaven,
hallowed be thy name;
thy kingdom come;
thy will be done on earth as it is in heaven.
Give us this day our daily bread;
and forgive us our trespasses
as we forgive those who trespass against us;
and lead us not into temptation,
but deliver us from evil.
Amen.

Hail Mary

Hail, Mary, full of grace,
the Lord is with you!
Blessed are you among women,
and blessed is the fruit of your womb, Jesus.
Holy Mary, Mother of God,
pray for us sinners,
now and at the hour of our death.
Amen.

Glory to the Father (Doxology)

Glory to the Father,
and to the Son,
and to the Holy Spirit,
as it was in the beginning,
is now, and will be for ever.
Amen.

Resource Center

Background

The Sign of the Cross Tracing the cross on one's own body or the forehead of another has been a common Christian gesture since the early centuries of the Church. The words of this traditional prayer echo the Rite of Baptism.

The Lord's Prayer This prayer has its roots in Scripture. In the Gospels of Matthew *(Matthew 6:9–13)* and Luke *(Luke 11:2–4)*, Jesus teaches a form of this prayer to his disciples. In various forms this prayer is used by all Christians. The Lord's Prayer is prayed at Mass, in communal celebrations of the Sacrament of Reconciliation, and as part of the Rosary.

The Hail Mary The first part of this prayer was used as an antiphon in the Little Office of Our Lady, a form of the Liturgy of the Hours prayed during the Middle Ages. The antiphon combines the Archangel Gabriel's greeting at the Annunciation *(Luke 1:26–28)* with Elizabeth's words of praise for Mary's motherhood *(Luke 1:42)*. The second part of the prayer was added as devotion to Mary grew.

Glory to the Father This ancient prayer of praise is part of the Rosary and is used to conclude the praying or chanting of a psalm in the Liturgy of the Hours.

I Confess (Confiteor)

I confess to almighty God,
and to you, my brothers and sisters,
that I have sinned through my own fault
in my thoughts and in my words,
in what I have done,
and in what I have failed to do;
and I ask blessed Mary, ever virgin,
all the angels and saints,
and you, my brothers and sisters,
to pray for me to the Lord our God.

Act of Contrition

My God,
I am sorry for my sins with all my heart.
In choosing to do wrong
and failing to do good,
I have sinned against you
whom I should love above all things.
I firmly intend, with your help,
to do penance,
to sin no more,
and to avoid whatever leads me to sin.
Our Savior Jesus Christ
suffered and died for us.
In his name, my God, have mercy.

The Jesus Prayer

Lord Jesus, Son of God,
have mercy on me, a sinner.
Amen.

I Confess (Confiteor)

- Explain to the children that many older Catholics know this prayer by its Latin name, which means "I confess."
- Remind the children that this prayer is sometimes used as part of the penitential rite at Mass.
- Show the children how to perform the ancient gesture of striking the breast at the words "through my own fault." This gesture of tapping the chest above the heart with a closed fist is a sign of sorrow for sin and humble acceptance of responsibility.

Act of Contrition

- Tell the children that this is a commonly used form of the prayer the penitent prays during the individual celebration of Reconciliation.
- If the children have not already done so, have them make prayer cards with the words of this prayer to use as reminders.
- Explain to the children that any of the prayers on this page may be used as an Act of Contrition.

The Jesus Prayer

- Tell the children that this short prayer, based on the words of a blind beggar seeking healing from Jesus, is often used to express sorrow for sin.
- Suggest that the children memorize this prayer.

Background

I Confess This prayer, in one form or another, has been part of the Church's liturgy since the Middle Ages. Once a part of the prayers at the foot of the altar recited by the priest as a sign of personal humility and unworthiness, the prayer has been refashioned into an eloquent act of contrition that recognizes the communal nature of the penitential journey.

Act of Contrition In addition to this text, the Rite of Penance offers eight other Acts of Contrition, plus the Jesus Prayer, as options. Three of the optional texts are drawn from Scriptural statements of penitence: *Psalm 25:6–7*; *Psalm 50:4–5*; and

Luke 15:18, 18:13. The penitent is also free to express contrition and a purpose of amendment in his or her own words.

The Jesus Prayer This prayer in its present form comes from the Orthodox tradition, where it is still in frequent use. At one time it was associated with a type of contemplative prayer known as *Hesychasm*, or "the prayer of the heart," which involved repetition of the prayer coordinated with breathing.

Our Moral Guide

These pages contain important information for the children to use in examining their conscience and making good choices. Help the children become familiar with this material.

The Great Commandment

Review this central commandment with the children as Jesus might have heard the Scriptures reviewed in the synagogue. Pronounce each phrase slowly and meaningfully, and have the children repeat it after you in the same manner.

The Beatitudes

- Review the Beatitudes with the children. Remind the children that the word *beatitude* means "blessedness."

- Help the children understand what is meant by each of the qualities Jesus describes. (Some suggestions: *poor in spirit*—trusting in God; *mourn*—sharing others' sorrows; *meek*—humble, not boastful; *hunger and thirst for righteousness*—working for holiness and justice; *merciful*—forgiving, kind; *clean of heart*—honest, modest, prayerful; *peacemakers*—helping people settle differences; *persecuted for the sake of righteousness*—willing to stand up for what is right.) Then ask volunteers to suggest ways that the children may live these qualities in their everyday lives.

Our Moral Guide

The Great Commandment

"You shall love the Lord your God with all your heart, with all your soul, with all your strength, and with all your mind;
and your neighbor as yourself."

—Luke 10:27

The Beatitudes

"Blessed are the poor in spirit,
  for theirs is the kingdom of heaven.
Blessed are they who mourn,
  for they will be comforted.
Blessed are the meek,
  for they will inherit the land.
Blessed are they who hunger and thirst for righteousness,
  for they will be satisfied.
Blessed are the merciful,
  for they will be shown mercy.
Blessed are the clean of heart,
  for they will see God.
Blessed are the peacemakers,
  for they will be called children of God.
Blessed are they who are persecuted for the sake of righteousness,
  for theirs is the kingdom of heaven."

—Matthew 5:3–10

Resource Center

Scripture Background

- The **Great Commandment** appears in slightly different forms in two Gospels (**Matthew 22:37–39** and **Luke 10:27**). The version given here is Luke's. The Great Commandment was also stated in **Deuteronomy 6:4** and **Leviticus 19:18**. It remains an honored part of Jewish teaching.

- Christians traditionally give the title **Beatitudes** to the eight teachings of Jesus presented in **Matthew 5:3–10**. The formula "Blessed is the one who . . ." occurs often in Old Testament wisdom literature. Here, within the context of the Sermon on the Mount, Jesus uses a tradition familiar to his Jewish listeners to announce the values of God's kingdom.

Catechetical Background

For more on the place of the Great Commandment and the Beatitudes in guiding Christian morality and forming conscience, see the *Catechism of the Catholic Church* (#2055, the Great Commandment, and #1716–1729, the Beatitudes).

The Ten Commandments

1. **I am the Lord your God. You shall not have strange gods before me.**
   Put God first in your life before all things.

2. **You shall not take the name of the Lord your God in vain.**
   Respect God's name and holy things. Do not use bad language.

3. **Remember to keep holy the Lord's day.**
   Take part in the Mass on Sundays and holy days. Avoid unnecessary work on these days.

4. **Honor your father and your mother.**
   Obey and show respect to parents and others who are responsible for you.

5. **You shall not kill.**
   Do not hurt yourself or others. Take care of all life.

6. **You shall not commit adultery.**
   Show respect for marriage and family life. Respect your body and the bodies of others.

7. **You shall not steal.**
   Respect creation and the things that belong to others. Do not cheat.

8. **You shall not bear false witness against your neighbor.**
   Tell the truth. Do not gossip.

9. **You shall not covet your neighbor's wife.**
   Be faithful to family members and friends. Do not be jealous.

10. **You shall not covet your neighbor's goods.**
    Share what you have. Do not envy what other people have. Do not be greedy.

Our Moral Guide : 57

The Ten Commandments

- Review the Ten Commandments with the children. Be sure the children understand what each commandment requires of them.

- Make a class mural or sculpture of the tablets of the Ten Commandments. Put the first three commandments (love God) on the left tablet and the next seven commandments (love your neighbor) on the right tablet.

- Help the children develop an examination of conscience based on the Ten Commandments. Make sure the questions are appropriate to the children's ages and circumstances.

Scripture Background

The **Ten Commandments** are enumerated in **Exodus 20:2–17** and **Deuteronomy 5:6–21**. There are slight differences between the two forms, and neither is exactly consistent with the wording and numbering given here. The wording and numbering traditionally familiar to Catholics and Lutherans was devised by Saint Augustine; other Christian communities number the commandments differently. Even with these differences, however, the Ten Commandments continue to express the heart of God's law for all people.

Catechetical Background

Part III, Section Two of the *Catechism of the Catholic Church* is devoted to a detailed presentation of the relationship between the Ten Commandments and Christian moral life.

Precepts of the Church

- Review this list with the children. Be sure they understand how the precepts apply to their own circumstances.
- Go through the parish bulletin or diocesan newspaper with the children, pointing out examples of the precepts in action.

Works of Mercy

- Review these lists with the children.
- Invite the children to act out examples of how they might practice the works of mercy.

Precepts of the Church

1. Take part in the Mass on Sundays and holy days. Keep these days holy, and avoid unnecessary work.
2. Celebrate the Sacrament of Reconciliation at least once a year if there is serious sin.
3. Receive Holy Communion at least once a year during Easter time.
4. Fast and abstain on days of penance.
5. Give your time, gifts, and money to support the Church.

Works of Mercy

Corporal (for the body)
Feed the hungry.
Give drink to the thirsty.
Clothe the naked.
Shelter the homeless.
Visit the sick.
Visit the imprisoned.
Bury the dead.

Spiritual (for the spirit)
Warn the sinner.
Teach the ignorant.
Counsel the doubtful.
Comfort the sorrowful.
Bear wrongs patiently.
Forgive injuries.
Pray for the living and the dead.

58 : Our Moral Guide

Resource Center

Background

- The **precepts of the Church** reflect the rights and duties of all Catholics. The precepts (a word that means "teachings") have existed in some form since the fourth century, although the numbering and wording have changed through the years and have varied in different countries.
- The **works of mercy** are actions on behalf of those in physical, spiritual, and emotional need. They are drawn from Scripture (particularly the injunctions of the prophets and the actions of Jesus) and the Church's practice. Practicing works of mercy can be beneficial both as penance and as a strengthening of conscience.

Catechetical Background

For more on the place of the precepts of the Church in formation of conscience, see the *Catechism of the Catholic Church* (#2041–2042). For more on the works of mercy and other actions for justice in Christian moral life, see the *Catechism of the Catholic Church* (#2443–2449).

Examination of Conscience

1. Look at your life. Compare your actions and choices with the Beatitudes, the Ten Commandments, the Great Commandment, and the precepts of the Church.
2. Ask yourself:
   * When have I not done what God wants me to do?
   * Whom have I hurt?
   * What have I done that I knew was wrong?
   * What have I not done that I should have done?
   * Are there serious sins I did not mention the last time I confessed?
   * Have I done penance? Have I tried as hard as I could to make up for past sins?
   * Have I changed my bad habits?
   * Am I sincerely sorry for all my sins?
3. In addition to confessing your sins, you may want to talk to the priest about one or more of the above questions.
4. Pray for the Holy Spirit's help to change and start over.

Examination of Conscience : 59

Examination of Conscience

This page provides a sample format for an examination of conscience.

* Review these steps and questions with the children.
* Remind the children that this is a model to work from. Encourage the children to make up their own questions for an examination of conscience based on the Ten Commandments, the Beatitudes, and the precepts of the Church.
* Teach the children the traditional Prayer to the Holy Spirit ("Come, Holy Spirit . . ."), or help them compose their own prayers for the Holy Spirit's guidance and help.

Background

The practice of prayerfully reviewing one's life has been a part of Christian spirituality from the earliest days, having its roots in the Jewish tradition of individual and communal spiritual reflection. The desert monks, and later the Catholic monastic orders, developed the practice further. At times in the Church's history there has been an overemphasis on the legalistic aspects of sin, leading to rigid formulas ("laundry lists") for the examination of conscience. Today the emphasis has returned to a more balanced reflection on one's sins and failings with the firm intention to do better.

Catechetical Background

For more on the formation and examination of the Christian moral conscience, see the *Catechism of the Catholic Church* (#1776–1794). For a sample examination of conscience directed at adults, see Appendix III of the *Rite of Penance*.

Celebrating the Sacrament of Reconciliation

These pages describe the communal and individual forms of the Sacrament of Reconciliation. Use these pages for preparation and review. The material on these pages is also provided for the children in *My Reconciliation Book*, for their use during the period of preparation and afterward. As part of the children's preparation, you may use the material on these pages as the outline for a walkthrough of the children's First Reconciliation celebration.

Celebrating the Sacrament of Reconciliation

The Communal Rite of Reconciliation

- Before celebrating the Sacrament of Reconciliation, take time to examine your conscience. Pray for the Holy Spirit's help.

1. **Introductory Rites**
   Join in singing the opening hymn. The priest will greet the assembly and lead you in the opening prayer.

2. **Reading from Scripture**
   Listen to the word of God. There may be more than one reading, with a hymn or psalm in between. The last reading will be from one of the Gospels.

3. **Homily**
   Listen as the priest helps you understand the meaning of the Scriptures.

4. **Examination of Conscience with Litany of Contrition and the Lord's Prayer**
   After the homily there will be a time of silence. The priest may lead the assembly in an examination of conscience. This is followed by the prayer of confession and the litany or song. Then all will pray the Lord's Prayer together.

5. **Individual Confession, Giving of Penance, and Absolution**
   While you wait your turn to talk with the priest, you may pray quietly or join in singing. When it is your turn, confess your sins to the priest. He will talk to you about how to do better and give you a penance. Then the priest will pray the prayer of absolution.

6. **Closing Rite**
   After everyone has confessed individually, join in singing or praying a song or litany of thanksgiving. The priest will lead the closing prayer and bless the assembly. Then the priest or deacon will dismiss the assembly.

- After celebrating the sacrament, carry out your penance as soon as possible.

60 : Celebrating the Sacrament of Reconciliation

Resource Center

Link to Liturgy

The Rite of Penance provides a wide range of optional prayers and readings for use in celebrations of the Sacrament of Reconciliation. The rite also provides sample penitential services, including one designed specifically for children. You may wish to review some of the optional prayer texts with the children or arrange to celebrate a penitential service as part of the children's preparation for the sacrament.

The Individual Rite of Reconciliation

- Before celebrating the Sacrament of Reconciliation, take time to examine your conscience. Pray for the Holy Spirit's help.
- Wait for your turn to enter the Reconciliation room.
- You may meet with the priest face-to-face or be separated from the priest by a screen.

1. **Welcome**
   The priest will welcome you and invite you to pray the Sign of the Cross.
2. **Reading from Scripture**
   The priest may read or recite a passage from the Bible. You may be invited by the priest to read the Scripture yourself.
3. **Confession of Sins and Giving of Penance**
   Tell your sins to the priest. The priest will talk with you about how to do better. Then the priest will give you a penance.
4. **Act of Contrition**
   Pray an Act of Contrition.
5. **Absolution**
   The priest will hold his hand over your head and pray the prayer of absolution. As he says the final words, he will make the Sign of the Cross.

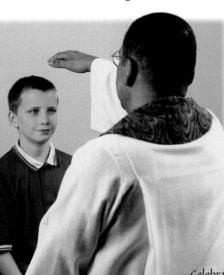

6. **Closing Prayer**
   The priest will pray, "Give thanks to the Lord, for he is good." You answer, "His mercy endures for ever." Then the priest will dismiss you.

- After celebrating the sacrament, carry out your penance as soon as possible.

Celebrating the Sacrament of Reconciliation : 61

Catechetical Background

For more on the theology and practice of the Sacrament of Reconciliation, see the *Catechism of the Catholic Church* (#1422–1484).

Glossary

This section gives the children a visual reference for some key terms associated with the Sacrament of Reconciliation.

- Throughout the children's preparation for First Reconciliation, refer to this section to enhance their understanding of the celebration.

- Invite the children to draw their own illustrations for some of the terms.

- Take the children on a tour of the parish church. Ask the sacristan or another parish minister to show the children the Reconciliation room, chapel, or confessional. Allow the children to become comfortable with the furnishings of the room. Show the children how the main church is set up for communal celebrations of the sacrament.

- Go through the glossary, word by word, asking the children to provide definitions in their own words.

Illustrated Glossary

absolution
(ab•suh•LOO•shuhn): The forgiveness of sin we receive from God through the Church in the Sacrament of Reconciliation. The word *absolve* means "to wash away."

communal celebration
(kuh•MYOO•nuhl seh•luh•BRAY•shuhn): One form of celebrating the Sacrament of Reconciliation. In a communal celebration the assembly gathers to pray and hear God's word. Each penitent then confesses, receives a penance, and is absolved privately.

confession
(kuhn•FEH•shuhn): Telling our sins to a priest in the Sacrament of Reconciliation. What we confess to the priest is private.

contrition
(kuhn•TRIH•shuhn): Sorrow for sins and a willingness to do better. Contrition is our first step toward forgiveness. As part of the Sacrament of Reconciliation, we pray an **Act**, or Prayer, **of Contrition**.

62 : Glossary

Resource Center

Catechetical Background

For more on the people, places, and things associated with the celebration of the Sacrament of Reconciliation, see the Introduction to the *Rite of Penance*.

examination of conscience

(ig•ZA•muh•NAY•shuhn UHV KAHNT•shuhnts):
A prayerful way of looking at our lives in light
of the Ten Commandments, the Beatitudes, the
life of Jesus, and the teachings of the Church.

individual celebration

(in•duh•VIJ•wuhl seh•luh•BRAY•shuhn): One form of
celebrating the Sacrament of Reconciliation. In an
individual celebration the penitent meets with the priest
in private. The penitent then confesses, receives a
penance, and is absolved privately.

penance

(PEH•nuhnts): Prayers and actions done to make up for
the harm our sins have caused. In the Sacrament of
Reconciliation, the priest gives us a penance to do. The
celebration of the Sacrament of Reconciliation is called
the **Rite of Penance**.

penitent

(PEH•nuh•tuhnt): The person who confesses his or her
sins to the priest in the Sacrament of Reconciliation.

priest

(PREEST): A man who is ordained to serve God and the Church by celebrating the sacraments, preaching, and presiding at Mass. The priest is the **confessor**, or minister of the Sacrament of Reconciliation. For the Sacrament of Reconciliation, the priest wears a stole. The **stole** is a sign of the priest's obedience to God and of his priestly authority.

Reconciliation room

(REH•kuhn•sih•lee•AY•shuhn ROOM): A room or chapel in which the confessor hears the penitent's confession of sins. The room is usually furnished with chairs, a kneeler, a table for the Bible and candle, and a movable screen that can be used as a divider between the priest and the penitent.

Scripture

(SKRIPT•sher): The word of God contained in the Bible. The word *scripture* means "holy writing." Scripture is used for reflecting on God's love and forgiveness in the Sacrament of Reconciliation. Scripture is proclaimed by a **lector**, or reader, at Mass or in other liturgical celebrations.

sin

(SIN): The choice to disobey God. Sin can be serious **(mortal)** or less serious **(venial)**. Sin is a deliberate choice, not a mistake or an accident. We accept God's loving forgiveness for our sins when we show by our sorrow that we are willing to do better.

Handouts and Activities

This section of the Teaching Guide contains reproducible pages that provide additional background or enrichment activities to supplement the lessons of *Celebrating Our Faith: Reconciliation*.

To share these pages with the children, follow these directions:

Pages HA2–HA4—The Prodigal Child

Duplicate pages HA3–HA4, and give copies to the children. Work with the children to act out the story, using suggestions found in Background Notes on page HA2.

Pages HA5–HA7—The Lost Sheep

Duplicate pages HA6–HA7, and give copies to the children. Work with the children to act out the story, using suggestions found in Background Notes on page HA5.

Pages HA8–HA10—Zacchaeus

Duplicate pages HA9–HA10, and give copies to the children. Work with the children to act out the story, using suggestions found in Background Notes on page HA8.

Page HA11—First Reconciliation Preparation Certificate

Duplicate this page, making a copy for each child. You may wish to make copies on parchment-like or colored paper. Help the children fill in the blanks, or get information from the children and have the certificates lettered by a calligrapher. Present the certificates at the last class session.

The Prodigal Child

based on Luke 15:11–32

Background Notes

Cast
- narrator (inner voice of prodigal child)
- prodigal child (son or daughter)
- father
- mother
- older brother or sister
- party guests (for two scenes)
- pigs

Costume Ideas
All "people" characters may wear simple cloth or paper tunics with rope or yarn belts. Some may wear bathrobes as outerwear. Veils for women and headdresses for men may be improvised from pillowcases and towels. Characters may wear sandals or be barefoot. The prodigal child should have a traveling cloak over a ragged tunic; the father should give the child a brightly colored robe as a gesture of welcome. Pigs can wear paper-plate masks and cardboard hooves.

Props
- traveling bundle or backpack for prodigal child
- party trays and pitchers
- straw or crumpled paper for pigsty
- cornhusks for pig food
- ring for father to give prodigal child
- colored robe

Setting
In this production the children are asked to mime as the narrator speaks. This dramatization has three areas of action: the family home, the city, and the pigsty. These should be indicated by setting scenes in three separate areas. The father and the prodigal child meet halfway between the pigsty and the family home.

The Prodigal Child

based on Luke 15:11–32

*As the play opens, the **prodigal child** is leaving the family home. The **father** and **mother** are sadly seeing the child off, while the **older child** works, pretending to be indifferent.*

Narrator: I remember the day I left home. I didn't care what my family said. I thought I was big enough and smart enough to do just as I pleased. My parents were sad, but I was happy. It was party time!

*The **prodigal child**, carrying pack, skips off toward the city. The **father** and **mother** watch, sad. When the **prodigal child** reaches the city, **party guests** surround him or her. They mime having a great time.*

Narrator: It didn't take me long to find friends. They helped me spend my father's money. We partied night and day.

*The **prodigal child** mimes being tired and lies down. **Party guests** steal the **prodigal child's** traveling cloak and pack and leave. The **prodigal child** wakes up, mimes a headache, and sees that friends and possessions are gone.*

Narrator: Maybe I wasn't so smart after all. Now I had no friends, no money, and no way to get a job. You won't believe where I ended up.

*The **prodigal child** mimes asking for jobs and being turned away. Finally, the **prodigal child** reaches the pigsty. The **pigs** act hungry. The **prodigal child**, sitting on the ground, begins dejectedly feeding cornhusks to the **pigs**. After a time the **prodigal child** mimes nibbling experimentally on a cornhusk.*

Narrator: Pigs! In my religion, pigs are unclean. We can't eat their meat or even be around them. But I had nowhere else to go. I was so hungry, even the pigs' food looked good to me.

*The **prodigal child** mimes falling asleep, crying. **Father**, **mother**, and **older child** come to stand around the sleeping **prodigal child**, reaching out their hands.*

Narrator: One night I dreamed about my home. When I awoke, I remembered how good my family had been to me. I felt sorry for leaving them. I thought about how well my father treated even the servants. "Maybe I'll go home," I thought. "Maybe I can get a job as my father's servant."

Father, mother, and older child return to the family home. The prodigal child wakes up, stretches, and feeds the last of the cornhusks to the pigs. The prodigal child pats a few pigs on the head to say good-bye, takes back one cornhusk for the road, and sets off toward home. As the prodigal child moves toward the home, the father moves toward the prodigal child. They meet halfway, and the prodigal child falls at the father's feet.

Narrator: I wasn't more than halfway home before I saw my father. He had come out to meet me. I felt so sorry. I knelt down at his feet and begged him to forgive me. I told him I wasn't worthy to be his child, but I could be a servant.

The father raises the prodigal child up and they embrace. The father takes a ring from his hand and puts it on the prodigal child's hand. The father leads the prodigal child home, where the mother waits to embrace the prodigal child. The father puts a bright robe on the prodigal child, and motions for party guests, who arrive and mime celebrating.

Narrator: My father forgave me. Not only that, he gave a party for me. It was a real party, with real friends. I was home.

Older child comes in from fields, looks startled by the party and the return of the prodigal child. Older child goes to father and mimes anger. Father puts arm around older child.

Narrator: My brother (sister) didn't understand. I don't blame him (her), because I didn't think I deserved a party either. But my father explained. "You are my own good child," he said. "I know everything you do, and I am proud of you. But of course we have to celebrate because it was like my other child was dead and has come back to life!" That's exactly what it felt like to me, too.

The prodigal child, older child, father, and mother join hands and smile.

The Lost Sheep

based on Luke 15:1–7

Background Notes

Cast
- good shepherd
- lost sheep
- other sheep (the "ninety-nine")
- wolf
- other shepherds

Costume Ideas
Shepherds may wear simple cloth or paper tunics with rope or yarn belts. Some may wear bathrobes as outerwear. Headdresses may be improvised from pillowcases and towels. Shepherds may wear sandals or be barefoot. The sheep (including the lost sheep) may wear white tunics, cardboard hooves, and paper-plate sheep masks with frames made from cotton balls. The lost sheep has a sign with the number 100 around its neck. The other sheep have signs with random numbers from 1–99. The wolf wears a paper-plate mask and a brown robe or tunic.

Props
- shepherds' crooks or staffs
- lanterns

Setting
If possible, perform this dramatization outside. You may indicate natural formations with cardboard cutouts of rocks, bushes, and campfire.

The Lost Sheep

based on Luke 15:1–7

*As the play opens, the **good shepherd** is leading the **sheep** (including the **lost sheep**). **Other shepherds** stand off in the distance. The **lost sheep** lingers behind all the rest, exploring behind bushes and daydreaming.*

*The **good shepherd** notices that the **lost sheep** has wandered away from the group.*

Good Shepherd: You, there! Number 100! What have I told you about sticking together?

*The **good shepherd** shoos the **lost sheep** back into the herd. The **wolf** enters and hides behind a bush, peeking out every so often to look at the **sheep**. Meanwhile, the **good shepherd** leads the **sheep** to where the **other shepherds** are miming standing or sitting around a campfire.*

Good Shepherd *(to the **sheep**)*: Settle down now, all of you. You can graze a little but don't stray away. That means you, Number 100! Remember there are wolves around.

*The **good shepherd** sits down at the campfire and mimes talking and eating with **other shepherds**. The **sheep** mime grazing on the grass. Some curl up to sleep. The **lost sheep** slowly drifts away from the group, heading toward the bush where the **wolf** waits.*

Wolf *(in a stage whisper)*: Here, sheepy, sheepy, sheepy! That's right, I mean you. Come on over. I won't hurt you. Why should you let that shepherd boss you around?

*The **lost sheep** moves closer to the **wolf**, timidly at first but then more confidently. As the **lost sheep** gets closer to the **wolf**, the **lost sheep** turns back and waves good-bye in the **good shepherd's** direction.*

Wolf *(to **lost sheep**)*: All right! Come on, let me show you where to have a good time. Are you hungry?

*The **lost sheep** nods. The **wolf** looks at the **lost sheep**.*

Wolf: Mmmmm. Me, too.

*The **wolf** leads the **lost sheep** out of sight behind a bush. Meanwhile, the **other shepherds** have settled down to sleep. The **good shepherd** makes one last count of his **sheep**.*

Good Shepherd: . . . 97, 98, 99. Oh, wait a minute. That can't be right. Where's Number 100. Number 100! Number 100! Don't trick me by hiding again! This is no time to fool around!

*The **good shepherd's** shouting wakes up the **other shepherds** and the **sheep**. The **sheep** baa anxiously.*

Other Shepherds: Hey, what's going on? Keep it down, will you?

Good Shepherd: Number 100 is missing. I've got to find it.

Other Shepherds: Oh, come on. Are you kidding? Number 100 is **always** lost. Give it up. You've got 99 sheep right here.

*The **good shepherd** takes a lantern and a shepherd's crook. He moves off to look for the **lost sheep**. The **other shepherds** sit up, grumbling.*

Good Shepherd: I'm in charge of all my sheep. I don't give up on any of them—even Number 100.

*As the **good shepherd** looks for the **lost sheep**, the **lost sheep** comes out from behind a bush, running from the **wolf**. The **wolf**, who has given up pretending to be nice, chases the **lost sheep**. Finally the **good shepherd** steps between the **wolf** and the **lost sheep**, holding up the lantern and the shepherd's crook, looking fierce. The **lost sheep** curls up in a frightened ball at the **good shepherd's** feet. The **wolf** freezes, then slowly backs away out of sight.*

Good Shepherd: Come on, Number 100. Let's go back where you belong. You know I'd never let a wolf get you. Now don't stray again, all right?

*The **lost sheep** baas obediently, relieved. The **good shepherd** leads the **lost sheep** back to the campfire, where the **other sheep** greet it happily. The **good shepherd** mimes passing some food to the **other shepherds**.*

Good Shepherd: Celebrate with me, friends! I have found the sheep that was lost!

Zacchaeus

based on Luke 19:1–10

Background Notes

Cast
• Zacchaeus

• Jesus

• disciples

• townspeople

Costume Ideas
All characters may wear simple cloth or paper tunics with rope or yarn belts. Some may wear bathrobes as outerwear. Veils for women and headdresses for men may be improvised from pillowcases and towels. Characters may wear sandals or be barefoot. Zacchaeus's clothing should be of a richer, better quality than that of other characters.

Props
• tax collector's table and stool

• play money

• sturdy, safe stepladder for "tree"

Setting
There are three areas of action: Zacchaeus's tax-collecting station, the tree, and Zacchaeus's house. Indicate these by staging the dramatization in three separate areas. If possible, do the dramatization outdoors, but do not let the child playing Zacchaeus climb a real tree or climb any higher than the steps of a sturdy stepladder.

Zacchaeus

based on Luke 19:1–10

*As the play begins, **Zacchaeus** the tax collector is seated at his table. A line of **townspeople** wait to pay taxes.*

Zacchaeus *(to first person in line):* That will be, let me see, uh . . . all the money you have with you.

*The **townsperson** groans and empties pockets of play money onto Zacchaeus's table. **Zacchaeus** takes half the money and hides it in his own tunic. As the **townsperson** walks sadly away, the other **townspeople** in line give him sympathy. They all look at **Zacchaeus** with anger.*

Townspeople: That Zacchaeus! It's bad enough we have to pay taxes, but he takes more than we owe. He's nothing but a thief.

*As the next person in line steps up to the table, **Jesus** and his **disciples** enter, followed by more **townspeople**. All attention turns to them.*

Townspeople: Look! It's Jesus, the carpenter's son from Nazareth. They say he's a great prophet. He heals the sick. He even forgives sinners in God's name.

*One by one, **townspeople** leave the tax line and go to join the crowd around **Jesus**. **Jesus** mimes talking to people and blessing them. The **disciples** bring townspeople forward for **Jesus** to help. **Zacchaeus** is left alone.*

Zacchaeus: Hey, wait! Where are you people going? I don't care if the messiah himself has come—you still have to pay your taxes!

*No one listens. **Zacchaeus** slowly pockets all the money on the table. He gets up and, pretending not to be interested, moves nearer to the crowd.*

Jesus *(to the **townspeople**):* Sell what you have, and give your money to those who are poor. That way you will have money bags that never wear out. You will have treasure in heaven that no thief can steal. Because where your real treasure is, that is where you will find your heart.

*Zacchaeus puts his hand on his heart. He stands thinking for a minute and bows his head. Then he tries to push closer to **Jesus**, but he can't see over the **townspeople**.*

Zacchaeus *(to himself)*: Real treasure? What does he mean? If this man Jesus can forgive sinners, can he even forgive a thief like me? If only I could see him! I'm so short. I know! I'll climb this sycamore tree.

*Zacchaeus climbs the stepladder. **Jesus** looks up at him and smiles.*

Jesus: Zacchaeus! Friend! Come down from there! I'm coming to have lunch with you today!

*Zacchaeus looks startled. The **disciples** and **townspeople** look shocked and angry.*

Townspeople: Lunch with a sinner? What kind of prophet is this?

Disciples *(to **Jesus**)*: Lord, are you sure? We hear very bad things about this Zacchaeus. He works for the Romans! He steals from his own people!

*Jesus ignores them. He reaches out his hand to **Zacchaeus**, who slowly climbs down and leads **Jesus** off toward his home. The **disciples** and the **townspeople** follow. When they reach his house, Zacchaeus stops. He stands up straight and speaks in a loud voice.*

Zacchaeus: Lord, I'm a very rich man. But I'm not very happy. I want to find this real treasure you talk about. So starting right now, I'm giving half of everything I have to people who need it. And all of you I cheated—I'm paying you back, four times what I stole. I know you don't like me very much, but if you can forgive me, you're all welcome to have lunch.

*The **townspeople** and **disciples** cheer. They shake Zacchaeus's hand. He starts passing out paper money to everyone.*

Jesus: Today salvation has come to this house!

The Lord is merciful!
He is kind and patient,
and his love never fails.
—Psalm 103:8

The child of God,

_____ ,
(name)

a member of Christ's Body,
has completed the preparation for First Reconciliation,
and will celebrate this sacrament of God's love,
forgiveness, and mercy on

_____
(date)

at

_____ .
(name of church)

Signed,

_____
(prayer partner)

_____
(pastor or parish priest)

_____
(catechist)

First Reconciliation Family Retreat

The First Reconciliation Family Retreat is an opportunity for children who are celebrating First Reconciliation to explore the sacrament and its meaning with a parent or another adult. Many parents want to share the First Reconciliation experience with their child but are not certain how to do this. Children, too, want to understand the sacrament and share that understanding with a person they care about.

This retreat is designed to bring children and adults together. The environment will stimulate thought and discussion about the meaning of the Sacrament of Reconciliation and about how this sacrament fits within the Catholic faith.

The retreat also provides a parish-wide opportunity for personal growth, because the people involved in putting on the retreat will gain understanding of the sacrament as they prepare for and implement the retreat activities. For this reason, you may want to consider establishing a parish-wide committee to work on the retreat. Another possibility would be to use members of an existing parish committee, such as an education commission, to assist you.

The First Reconciliation Family Retreat pages contain preparation, activities, and handouts. The Director of Religious Education or a First Reconciliation catechist can begin with the preparation section and continue through the other two sections to follow the retreat as it is written.

There is some flexibility in scheduling the retreat. Although it is recommended that the retreat activities be conducted in one session, you may explore several options for the timing of that session.

Whenever you choose to schedule the retreat, it is very important to solicit support not only from the Reconciliation candidates and their families but also from catechists and the parish at large. Sample bulletin announcements and a letter to parents are included to assist you in gaining this support. The time line on page R2 will guide you in sharing this information in a timely fashion.

Finally, remember that the most important ingredient for the success of this retreat is your own enthusiasm. Remember that you are increasing understanding of Reconciliation in the children, their families, and the entire parish. No small feat!

Time Line

Timing	Tasks
Beginning of school year	Acquaint pastoral staff with retreat idea and gain approval from necessary persons to conduct retreat; determine whether to follow the one-day or two-day plan; consult with facilities scheduler to reserve needed space; add retreat to yearly schedule provided to all families; reserve videos you plan to borrow from diocesan library.
Two months before retreat	Run bulletin announcements to solicit volunteers and remind Reconciliation candidates and families of retreat dates.
Six weeks before retreat	If you do not have enough volunteers to assist with the retreat, start networking to find more.
One month before retreat	Check available supplies; order supplies that are not on hand; send home parent letter; verify videotape reservation.
Three weeks before retreat	Meet with volunteer session leaders to go over retreat plan, make specific assignments, and distribute activity plans; run bulletin announcements acquainting parish with the purpose of the retreat and asking for their support through prayer.
Two weeks before retreat	Check status on any supply orders; check on return of family reservation forms; contact families who have not responded; make necessary copies; fill folders; make name tags; make door signs for session rooms; select readers for prayer services and give them their parts to practice.
One week before retreat	Check on any outstanding supplies; meet with facilities planner to go over room requirements and specific setup arrangements; call volunteers to answer any questions and see if they need assistance with any aspect of their duties.
Day before retreat	Pick up videos; supervise room arrangements; distribute supplies to places where they will be used.
Retreat day	Arrive early to greet volunteers and direct Reconciliation candidates and companions; visit sessions to make certain that all run smoothly.
Day after retreat	Write thank-you notes to volunteers and others who contributed to the success of the retreat; inventory and store leftover supplies; tally evaluations.
One week after retreat	Meet with volunteers, family representatives, and others involved in the retreat to evaluate it and make notes for next year.

eeds

People

Adult companion for each child   Ideally, this would be a parent, but family circumstances may be such that other relatives will participate with the child. In some cases, neighbors or parents of other candidates may be able to go through the retreat with a child. It may be necessary to ask members of the parish to accompany children who would have no other companions.

Retreat staff   Suggested staffing for each activity is listed on the activity sheet. Additional personnel include:

   Retreat director   DRE, school principal, or program director who plans retreat and is on hand to see that all runs smoothly during the retreat.

   General volunteers   One or two people to direct participants as they arrive; prepare the room for prayer services; coordinate serving of snacks and meals, and so on.

Facilities

You will need a large room that will accommodate all participants for the opening and closing prayer services. Tables near the entry should hold name tags, folders, and registration lists. If you have decided to divide participants into small groups, color-code the name tags and assign each group a table in this room. You will also need one or two large classrooms or meeting rooms and access to a gymnasium or activity room.

Supplies

In addition to the supplies listed for each activity (see activity sheets), you will need some general supplies.

General Supplies

- folders (one per child-adult pair)
- name tags (color-coded for each small group, if necessary)
- signs for activity room doors
- handouts (prayer services, child's booklet, discussion questions, schedule, evaluation sheet)
- snacks for welcome
- candles and matches (one large candle for opening prayer; one vigil light in a glass container for each family for closing prayer) (**Note:** If fire regulations prohibit this, use candelabra or candlesticks. Place these in the sanctuary or front of the room and have each child-adult pair light one.)
- banner stand for closing prayer service
- musicians or soft, recorded music for closing prayer service

General Remarks

Bulletin Announcements

Your parish bulletin can be used to help recruit volunteers and remind parents of the retreat. Sample announcements follow:

> **Can you help us share God's love? Volunteers are needed for this year's First Reconciliation Family Retreat on *[date]*. We can use people with all skill levels and will assign you to an activity based on your interest and experience. Please call *[name and phone number]* for more information.**

> **Parents are reminded that the First Reconciliation Retreat will be held on *[date]* at *[time]* at *[place]*.**

> **Your prayers are requested for the success of the retreat that our First Reconciliation class will experience on *[date]*.**

Photographs

To help the children remember the retreat and to inform the parish about the activities, you may want to assign a volunteer to take pictures during the retreat. This volunteer can move from activity to activity, taking photographs of as many children and adults as possible. After the photographs are developed, arrange them on a sheet of poster board and display them in a prominent place in the church or school.

Follow-Up Meeting

After a major project such as this retreat, it is very tempting to proclaim it a success and plan to follow the same pattern next year. However, you may want to hold a follow-up meeting to find out what the parish staff and volunteers observed at the retreat. Consider making changes based on those observations and the participants' evaluations. Questions you may want to discuss at the meeting include:

- Was the schedule appropriate for the activities?
- Were children and adults engaged in the activities?
- Was the room arrangement adequate?
- Were there any difficulties in moving from activity to activity?
- Did volunteers receive adequate training and support?
- Should any activities be added or taken out?
- What were our successes? Where can we improve?

Schedule

In planning the retreat, the retreat director may wish to consider the following guidelines:

- The optimal number of children in a small group is seven to ten.
- Parishes with a very large Reconciliation class can either schedule retreats for portions of the class on different days or have more than one group doing an activity at a time. Of course, each parish's facilities and volunteer situation will come into play here, and the retreat director may need to adjust the schedule accordingly.

Here is a sample schedule for a weekend afternoon retreat:	
12:30	Arrival, distribute name tags and folders, conduct Opening Prayer Service
1:00	Adults to Activity 1a; children to Activity 1b; begin Session 1
1:40	Session 2
2:10	Session 3
2:40	Session 4
3:10	Gather together for final remarks and Closing Prayer Service (allow 20 minutes)

Here is a sample schedule for a two-part evening retreat, incorporating the celebration of Reconciliation:	
Day 1	
6:30	Arrival, distribute name tags and folders, conduct Opening Prayer Service
7:00	Session 2
7:30	Session 3
8:00	Session 4
8:30	Closing Prayer Service (allow 20 minutes)
Day 2	
7:00	Arrival, distribute name tags and folders
7:10	Adults to Activity 1a; children to Activity 1b; begin Session 1
7:50	Reception of the Sacrament of Reconciliation (optional)

Sample group rotation, with participants divided into three small groups:

Group	Session 2	Session 3	Session 4
Group A	Activity 2	Activity 3	Activity 4
Group B	Activity 3	Activity 4	Activity 2
Group C	Activity 4	Activity 2	Activity 3

Note: All groups meet together for Session 1 (Activity 1a for adults; Activity 1b for children).

# Activity 1a

Adult Education (40 minutes)

Purpose
- To supply background information on preparing children for First Reconciliation
- To acquaint adults with procedures for the parish celebration

Presenters
- DRE or parish school principal for parish information
- Volunteer to moderate discussion

Room
Conference room or large classroom

Preparation
- Select video.
- Prepare handouts with discussion questions and specific information needed for parish celebration.

Materials
- video on the Sacrament of Reconciliation, such as *Celebrating Reconciliation with Families* (produced by Salt River Production Group; BROWN-ROA)
- TV and videocassette player
- handouts as appropriate for parish information

Procedure
1. Leader discusses the history and theology of Reconciliation (or reviews key points if pastor has already done this).
2. Show and discuss video.
3. Allow time for adult discussion.
4. DRE or school principal discusses practices and procedures for parish celebration (if this has not already been covered by the pastor).

© BROWN-ROA

Retreat Director: Duplicate this page. Clip off this portion, and make copies for those in charge of Activity 1a.

# Activity 1b

Reviewing the Ceremony and Practicing Music
(40 minutes)

Purpose
To familiarize the children with the songs and prayers that will be used at their First Reconciliation celebration

Presenters
Catechist and parish music minister, music teacher, or organist

Room
Music room or classroom

Preparation
- Select songs to teach the children for use at the Reconciliation service. (BROWN-ROA's *Celebrating Our Faith* CD and cassette contain several possibilities.)
- Obtain copies of songs and prayer texts. (**Note:** Do not duplicate copyrighted music or prayer texts from the *Rite of Penance* without the publisher's permission.)

Supplies
- copies of the *Rite of Penance* or *My Reconciliation Book*
- song sheets, hymnals, or missalettes
- piano, guitar, or other musical accompaniment
- recorded versions of songs and CD or tape player, if necessary

Procedure
1. Review with the children the order of celebration for their First Reconciliation. Take a few moments to go through each prayer.
2. Spend extra time with the Act of Contrition, helping the children memorize a standard prayer text or guiding them to compose their own.
3. Teach the children one or more songs that will be used for the First Reconciliation celebration.

Retreat Director: Duplicate this page. Clip off this portion, and make copies for those in charge of Activity 1b.

ctivity 2

Creating a Banner (30 minutes)

Purpose
- To acquaint the children and their families with symbols of Reconciliation
- To prepare a special presentation to the parish community

Presenter
Catechists or volunteers

Room
Classroom or meeting room

Supplies
- symbols of Reconciliation (lamb with shepherd's crook, heart, cross, tablets of the Ten Commandments, and so on) (**Note:** You may wish to display the images shown on the six *Celebrating Our Faith: Reconciliation* Sharing Pages.)
- felt or burlap for banner, felt squares or sheets of colored paper for each family, fabric markers, scissors, fabric glue or masking tape
- photographs of the children as requested in family letter

Preparation
- Display the Reconciliation symbols.
- Make available the children's photographs.
- Prepare large piece of felt or burlap for banner.

Procedure
1. Direct attention to the Reconciliation symbols. Lead the group in a discussion of the meaning of these symbols. Encourage volunteers to suggest other symbols.
2. Invite the children to choose their favorite symbol. Supply art materials, and have the adults help the children design individual felt squares or paper panels incorporating their favorite symbols and their photographs. Be sure everyone signs their work.
3. Help families place their completed pieces on the banner, but do not attach the pieces yet. (Volunteers will do this while families are working on another activity.) Explain that the completed banner will be displayed at the closing prayer service and then presented to the parish to display until the First Reconciliation celebration.

Retreat Director: Duplicate this page. Clip off this portion, and make copies for those in charge of Activity 2.

ctivity 3

Learning from a Video (30 minutes)

Purpose

To stimulate discussion of concepts presented in videos

Presenter

Catechist, religion teacher, or volunteer

Room

Classroom or meeting room

Supplies

- TV and videocassette player
- one or more videos with Reconciliation themes, such as *Celebrating Reconciliation with Children*, Segments 2 and 5 (produced by Salt River Production Group; BROWN-ROA), *Skateboard* (Franciscan Communications/St. Anthony Messenger Press), *The Prodigal* (BROWN-ROA), or *The Parable of the Lost Sheep* (produced by Twenty-Third Publications; BROWN-ROA).

Preparation

- Preview and select video(s) that will suit the parish's needs.
- Review discussion guide(s) for suggestions.

Procedure

1. Introduce the video(s), using strategies from the discussion guide(s).
2. Show the video(s).
3. Use the discussion guide(s) to review major points and enhance group understanding.

Retreat Director: Duplicate this page. Clip off this portion, and make copies for those in charge of Activity 3.

ctivity 4

Making a Cross (30 minutes)

Purpose
To emphasize the place of the cross in forgiveness and redemption

Presenters
Catechists or volunteers

Room
Classroom or meeting room

Preparation
- Prepare a cardboard cross shape (9″ high, 7″ wide, with cross arms 4″ across) for each child-adult pair. Cut shallow V-shaped notches into the ends of all four cross arms.
- Assemble a sample matchstick cross to serve as a model for the group. (See *Procedure*, below.)

Supplies
- one cardboard cross, prepared as above, for each child-adult pair
- one box of wooden stick matches (approximately 2″ long) for each child-adult pair
- one foil pie tin or small foil cookie sheet for each child-adult pair
- tacky glue

Procedure
1. Explain to the participants that the cross is a symbol of Christ's love for us. Every time we see a cross, we are reminded that Jesus sacrificed himself on a cross for our sins.
2. Give each pair a cardboard cross. Have each child write his or her name on one side (which will be the back) of the cross.
3. Have the adults, working carefully and quickly, light and blow out each match in their boxes, setting the burned matches on the foil tin or sheet to cool.
4. Have the adults determine when the matches are cool enough to handle. Ask them to shake any loose charcoal onto the foil tins.
5. Have the adults help the children spread glue on the cardboard cross shape, working with one cross arm at a time. Use the model you made to show the participants how to lay the matches, burned ends in, in a two-row herringbone pattern on the surface of the cross, following the diagonal of the V-shaped notches. (The Vs made by the matchsticks should meet in an X-shape at the center of the cross.)
6. Allow the crosses to dry. Make the completed crosses available for the children to pick up after the Closing Prayer Service.

Retreat Director: Duplicate this page. Clip off this portion, and make copies for those in charge of Activity 4.

# Sample Family Letter

Use this letter as a model for your own. Insert information specific to your retreat, and tailor the descriptions to the activities you will be doing. A sample tear-off-and-return response form is also included in this model.

[date]

Dear First Reconciliation Family,

As a way of helping prepare your child to celebrate First Reconciliation, our parish staff will be presenting a retreat for First Reconciliation candidates and their adult companions. We would like each child to come with a parent, a relative, or another special adult. During the retreat the children and their adult companions will explore the importance of Reconciliation and its meaning in their lives.

Activities during the retreat will include viewing and discussing videos, making a Reconciliation banner, and making a cross. There will also be a special adults-only session that will discuss preparing children for First Reconciliation. The parish staff and several volunteers have spent many hours preparing what we hope will be an enjoyable experience for all participants.

We have scheduled the retreat for *[date and time]* in *[location]*.

For one of our projects, we will need a small photograph of your child. A school picture or snapshot will be fine. These will be attached to a banner that will be displayed in the church.

Please return the attached form indicating your plans for the retreat. We are looking forward to seeing you at the retreat!

Sincerely,

[DRE, Pastor, Catechist, or Retreat Director]

First Reconciliation Retreat

Child's name _____

Adult companion's name _____

_____ We will be attending the retreat.
_____ We will not be attending the retreat.

# Child's Booklet

You may want to prepare a booklet for each child to work on during the retreat. This will give the children a special memento of their experience and will serve as an additional activity for the children who finish early. It will also provide space for children to sketch designs for their banner symbols.

Use three $5\frac{1}{2}'' \times 8\frac{1}{2}''$ sheets of paper for each booklet. After you have typed or printed the information for each page and duplicated the pages, bind them with staples close to the left edge of the front cover. Pages should contain the following information, with space left for drawings or writing. (Be sure to tailor the activity descriptions to suit your retreat.)

Page 1 (cover)
Our First Reconciliation Retreat

By _____

_____

Date _____

Page 2
We learned songs and prayers.
Write the words of the song or the Act of Contrition.

Page 3
We made a banner.
Draw your favorite Reconciliation symbol.

Page 4
We watched a video.
Draw a picture of your favorite scene from the video.

Page 5
We made a cross.
Write one sentence about what the cross means to you.

Page 6
We celebrated by lighting candles.
Draw a picture or write about your favorite part of the prayer services.

Catechists may wish to use the booklets in a follow-up activity after the retreat, or you may send the booklets home with families at the end of the retreat.

Opening Prayer Service

Sign of the Cross

Leader: Father, we gather today in your name to continue our preparation for the Sacrament of Reconciliation. Watch over us, and help us welcome our family and friends who have joined us to share their wisdom and support. As we begin our time with you, we light a candle to remind us of your Son, Jesus, the Light of the World. We ask that his light be with us today.

All: Amen.

(Leader lights the main candle.)

Child 1: God our Father, we have come to celebrate your unending love for us. Teach us to love one another as you love us.

All: Lord, have mercy.

Child 2: Jesus, Good Shepherd, help us follow your way of gentleness and mercy. Guide us along your path, even though it may be difficult.

All: Lord, have mercy.

Child 3: Holy Spirit, give us the courage to admit that we have done wrong and the strength to seek reconciliation.

All: Lord, have mercy.

Leader: Dear God, you have brought us together to help these young people grow in your love. Many people have guided their faith journey so far, and many will help them today. Grant us your wisdom in teaching these children and preparing them to celebrate your love and mercy in the Sacrament of Reconciliation.

Loving Father, look upon these children and help them joyfully learn of your great gift. Help them leave this retreat with greater understanding of and love for your sacraments, especially Reconciliation. We ask this through your Son, our Lord Jesus Christ.

All: Amen.

Sign of the Cross

Retreat Director: Duplicate this page. Clip off this portion, and make copies for all retreat participants.

Closing Prayer Service

Sign of the Cross or Opening Song

Leader: Dear God our Father, we return to this room where our retreat began, to think about what we have learned since we were here last. We come to praise you and thank you.

All: Amen.

Leader: Let us listen now to the message of our Father's forgiving love in the words of Jesus.

Reader: A story from the Gospel of Luke. (Have the children perform the Prodigal Child mime. [see pages HA2–HA4].)

Leader: Like the prodigal child in the story, may we recognize our faults, ask forgiveness, and celebrate our return to the Father's house. As a sign of our willingness to seek forgiveness and reconciliation from one another as from God, let us offer one another a sign of peace.

(Participants exchange a sign of peace.)

Leader: As we celebrate the completion of our retreat by displaying our Reconciliation banner, let us renew our baptismal commitment to the light of Christ by sharing the flame.
(As two volunteers bring in the Reconciliation banner and carry it solemnly to the banner stand, the leader and assistants light tapers and walk through the group lighting the vigil lights. The lit vigil lights should then be brought forth and placed on the altar or table while everyone sings "I Want to Walk as a Child of the Light" from BROWN-ROA's Celebrating Our Faith CD or cassette.)

Leader: Dear Father in heaven, may these candles remind us of the promises we made at Baptism. May they light the way to a renewed relationship with you and with our community in the Sacrament of Reconciliation. Send your Holy Spirit to guide these children and all your people, as we walk the way of peace. We ask this in the name of Jesus Christ, your Son.

All: Amen.

Sign of the Cross or Closing Song

Retreat Director: Duplicate this page. Clip off this portion, and make copies for all retreat participants.

valuation

We would like to know your opinion of the retreat. With your companion, please take a few minutes to fill out this paper. Give it to a staff member when you are done.

1. What was your overall feeling about the retreat?

   _____

   _____

2. Please circle a number to rate the following parts of the retreat, with 1 = not helpful and 5 = very good.

Activity 1a (Adult Education)	1	2	3	4	5
Activity 1b (Learning Prayers and Songs)	1	2	3	4	5
Activity 2 (Creating a Banner)	1	2	3	4	5
Activity 3 (Learning from a Video)	1	2	3	4	5
Activity 4 (Making a Cross)	1	2	3	4	5
Prayer Services	1	2	3	4	5
Child's Booklet	1	2	3	4	5

3. Adult: Do you feel that this retreat will help prepare your child for First Reconciliation? Why or why not?

   _____

   _____

4. Child: What was the most important thing you learned during the retreat? Why was it important to you?

   _____

   _____

Please write any additional comments. Thank you!

   _____

   _____

   _____

   _____

   _____

   _____

   _____

- -

Retreat Director: Duplicate this page. Clip off this portion, and make one copy for each child-adult pair. Distribute evaluation forms before the Closing Prayer Service.

Family Preparation Pages

This section is designed to provide support to families preparing children at home for First Reconciliation. This option may be exercised by families for a number of reasons, including

- the desire of parents to assume their full responsibility as the primary religious educators of their children.
- the need to prepare individual children who are out-of-cycle with the parish sacramental preparation program because of age difference, illness or disability, or time of joining the parish community.
- lack of resources within the parish for a sacramental preparation program.
- interest in forming neighborhood clusters, prayer groups, or basic Christian communities for sacramental preparation of children by families.

Home Lesson Plans

This section contains reproducible pages for parents and other family members to use with their children at home. Use of these pages presumes that each family will have a *Celebrating Our Faith: Reconciliation* child's book, a copy of *My Reconciliation Book*, and a set of *Sharing Pages*. The material in the home lesson plans is designed to be easy to use. These lesson plans do not require costly materials or large investments of time. Options are given for additional activities to extend the lessons should families so desire.

Catechetical Support

Although families using these pages at home will have what they need to prepare their children effectively for First Reconciliation, parish catechetical and pastoral staff should provide as much support as possible. Here are some ways you can support families preparing their children at home:

- Meet with families (whether it's one family or a neighborhood cluster) at the beginning of the preparation process. Give families their copies of *Celebrating Our Faith: Reconciliation*, *My Reconciliation Book*, *Sharing Pages*, and reproduced lesson plans. Let families know whom they may contact at the parish for ongoing support.
- Give families information about the practical details, such as obtaining baptismal certificates, and about your parish's schedule and guidelines for First Reconciliation celebrations (communal or individual celebration, for example). Clarifying these "housekeeping" details in advance can prevent misunderstandings.
- Be a liaison for families with your parish or diocesan resource library. Make useful books and videos (especially those recommended in the lesson plans) available for families to borrow.
- If possible, arrange for families to meet individually or as a group with the families of other children being prepared in the parish school or religious education program, as well as with the pastor, music minister, and other staff who will be involved in the First Reconciliation celebration. Be sure to include these families in the retreat.
- Reassure families that they are exercising their God-given ministry. Applaud their willingness to grow together in faith in this unique way.

CHAPTER 1
WE BELONG
Pages 6–13

See *Catechism of the Catholic Church, #1229–1233.*

Background The Sacraments of Initiation—Baptism, Confirmation, and Eucharist—make us members of the Church. Our initiation into the Paschal mystery of Christ's death and resurrection is not complete until we have celebrated all three of these sacraments. In the early centuries of the Church, the Sacraments of Initiation were celebrated at the same time, as they are today in the Rite of Christian Initiation of Adults and in some Eastern and Latin Rite communities. In the experience of most Latin Rite Catholics, Confirmation has become separated from Baptism and often occurs years after First Communion. But whenever the Sacraments of Initiation are celebrated, they form a unity that moves from the new birth of Baptism, through the anointing of the Holy Spirit in Confirmation, to the sharing in Christ's Body and Blood at the table of the Eucharist. "God's Spirit baptized each of us and made us part of the body of Christ" *(1 Corinthians 12:13).*

Preparing Your Child at Home

Getting Started
- Pray the opening prayer together, and read the text on pages 6 and 7. Talk about how each of the pictures represents a form of community.
- Supply construction paper and crayons or colored markers. Ask your child to draw the outline of your home on one sheet and the outline of your church on another. Make each outline large enough to fill the page. Write the name of your city above the outline of your house, and write the name of your church above its outline. Then, with the help of your child, write inside the house outline the names of some families who belong to your neighborhood community, and write inside the church outline the names of some families in your parish community. Discuss how many

names are in each picture. Discuss the names that are the same in the pictures. Next, show your child a map of the world. Help him or her locate the city in which you live. Then point to the whole map, and explain that our Catholic Church has members throughout the world. Ask your child how big the piece of paper would have to be to include the names of our whole Catholic community.

Sharing the Scriptures
- Read "We Are God's Children" on pages 8 and 9. Talk about how the pictures relate to the story.
- Talk about what it must have been like not to have known about Jesus or about the one true God. Then place yourselves in the crowd who heard Saint Paul's speech. Read the last paragraph on page 9 again, and explain to your child that just like the members of Paul's crowd who chose to include themselves in the family of God, we also choose to respond to God's gift of faith by becoming members of the Church.

Exploring the Rite
- Read the text on pages 10 and 11, including the *We Ask* question and answer. Point to each of the pictures as you read about the sacrament associated with it (from bottom right: Baptism, Confirmation, Eucharist). Discuss any questions your child may have.
- If you have photographs of family members celebrating any of the Sacraments of Initiation, show these to your child.
- *My Reconciliation Book*—Have your child fill out the personalization page of *My Reconciliation Book.* Take time over the course of this week to familiarize yourself with this booklet.

Living Reconciliation

- Read aloud the directions for the activity on page 12. Talk with your child again about community and about the Sacraments of Initiation. Then have your child complete the baptismal certificate. Find the information (date, church, godparents) and a photo before you begin. If you do not have a photo, help your child draw a picture representing his or her Baptism.

- Pray together "Children of One Family." Begin and end by making the Sign of the Cross together. If your child hasn't yet learned this, show him or her that it should be done slowly and with respect. You may want to read the main text of the prayer and have your child join with you for the "Hosanna in the highest!" refrain.

More to Share

- Volunteer for a local project that can help give your child an idea of the size of his or her community. Or, if possible, volunteer your child and yourself to be greeters at a parish Sunday Mass.

- *Sharing Page*—Complete the Chapter 1 *Sharing Page* together. It is intended as a review page, so you might notice some overlap. But it should work well to reinforce the chapter's key concepts.

- Books and Videos—You may wish to share these additional resources, available from the library, your diocesan media center, or publishers' catalogs.

For children and families

Celebrating Reconciliation with Children (6-part video series) (produced by Salt River Production Group; BROWN-ROA).

Segment 1: *We Belong* is designed for use with this chapter.

God Speaks to Us in Water Stories, by Mary Ann Getty-Sullivan (The Liturgical Press).

Scripture stories with water themes help children explore the symbols of Baptism.

For adults

A Child's Journey: The Christian Initiation of Children, by Rita Burns Senseman (St. Anthony Messenger Press).

A look at celebrating the Sacraments of Initiation with children of catechetical age.

What Makes Us Catholic? Discovering Our Catholic Identity (video) (Franciscan Communications/St. Anthony Messenger Press).

The beliefs and customs Catholics share.

Preparing for the Celebration

Read

"Christianity is more than a doctrine. It is Christ himself, living in those whom he has united to himself in one Mystical Body."

—*Thomas Merton*

Reflect

What does being a Christian mean to me?
How do I show that I am a member of the Body of Christ?

Pray

Jesus,
you have made me part of your own Body
in water and Spirit
and in the sacred Bread and Wine of
    the Eucharist.
Help me guide my child
to a fuller understanding of Christian life
and the mission to share your love.
Amen.

CHAPTER 2
WE CELEBRATE GOD'S LOVE
Pages 14–21

See Catechism of the Catholic Church, #1856–1857.

Background

Consciousness of sin is the fundamental impulse of contrition and reconciliation. Like the prodigal son, we "come to ourselves" and recognize how far we have come from our Father's house. Mortal and venial sin differ in degree of seriousness, but all personal sin has the same root—turning away from God's loving will for us, deciding in our pride that we know best. The Sacrament of Reconciliation is both reminder and celebration of the wonderful truth Jesus shared in the parable: when we acknowledge our sin and ask forgiveness, God meets us more than halfway. "The Lord is merciful! He is kind and patient, and his love never fails" *(Psalm 103:8).*

Preparing Your Child at Home

Getting Started

- Talk about ways each of you has, at times, hurt another person, and ways you have sought forgiveness. Discuss what might have happened if the person you hurt hadn't forgiven you.

- Pray the opening prayer together, and read the text on pages 14 and 15. Discuss what is happening in each of the photos.

Sharing the Scriptures

- When introducing your child to Reconciliation, it is important to explain that when we sin, God wants us to return to him in love and accept his mercy. To explain this, Jesus told the story of "The Forgiving Father." Read together the story on pages 16 and 17. Point out the illustrations, and talk about what the story means to each of you.

- When you have finished reading and discussing the story, make up a modern version of it. Take turns playing the role of the parent and the child.

Exploring the Rite

- Go through the boldfaced words on pages 18 and 19 with your child. Clarify any terms he or she doesn't understand.

- Read aloud "Our Second Chance" and the *We Ask* question and answer. Stop at any point where your child might have questions. Draw your child's attention to the photos, especially the picture of a communal Reconciliation celebration on page 18.

- *My Reconciliation Book*—Review page 2 with your child. You may want to talk with your child about your first celebration of the Sacrament of Reconciliation.

Living Reconciliation

- Help your child complete the exercise on page 20. Read the directions aloud, and remind your child about his or her responses to your discussions of this chapter's themes. Discuss and affirm your child's feelings.

- Pray together the prayer on page 21. Begin and end by making the Sign of the Cross. You might want to read the main text of the prayer and have your child join with you for the "Amen!" response.

More to Share

- Ask your child to draw or talk about examples of people sharing God's love. Ask him or her also to include a few examples of people choosing to ignore God's love. Talk about each example.

- *Sharing Page*—Complete the Chapter 2 *Sharing Page* together.

- Books and Videos—You may wish to share these additional resources, available from the library, your diocesan media center, or publishers' catalogs.

For children and families

Celebrating Reconciliation with Children (6-part video series) (produced by Salt River Production Group; BROWN-ROA).

    Segment 2: We Celebrate God's Love is designed for use with this chapter.

The Story of the Lost Son, by Tama M. Montgomery (Ideals Children's Books).

    The parable of the prodigal son retold for children.

For adults

Celebrating Reconciliation with Families (2-part video series) (produced by Salt River Production Group; BROWN-ROA).

    Father Joe Kempf helps parents reflect on the meaning of the sacrament.

Your Child's First Confession: Preparing for the Sacrament of Reconciliation (Liguori).

    An introduction to the sacrament for parents and families.

Preparing for the Celebration

Read

"Reconciliation sounds a large and theological term, but it simply means coming to ourselves and arising and going to our Father."

—*John Oman*

Reflect

When have I experienced true reconciliation in my life?

Who are the people who show me God's forgiving love?

Pray

Forgiving Father,
even when I wander away from your love,
you are there to meet me on the road home.
Keep me always open to your forgiveness
    and mercy,
and help me show my child
the way home to your constant love.
Amen.

CHAPTER 3
WE HEAR GOOD NEWS
Pages 22–29

See Catechism of the Catholic Church, #1349.

Background We meet God in the Scriptures. The inspired word of God is a living presence in the Christian community. In some form the word is shared in the celebration of each sacrament. The message of the Scriptures has special meaning in the context of Reconciliation. By reflecting on God's word, we measure our choices against the call to holiness. "Your word is a lamp that gives light wherever I walk" *(Psalm 119:105)*. We are reminded of the law of love. "Our Lord, your love is seen all over the world. Teach me your laws" *(Psalm 119:64)*. And we are encouraged to turn in contrition to the Lord, who is "kind and patient and always loving" *(Psalm 145:8)*.

Preparing Your Child at Home

Getting Started

- Talk with your child about all the different ways good news is shared (television, radio, newspaper, telephone, e-mail). Ask your child to recall some of the good news your family has received recently and how you have shared it. Many families have a special place around the house, such as the refrigerator door or a bulletin board, where family news is posted. You and your child may want to create or add to such a good news center.

- Pray the opening prayer, and read the text on pages 22 and 23. Before continuing, make sure your child understands the word *Scripture*. Thumb through a Bible with your child—drawing particular attention to the more commonly referred to books, such as Genesis, Psalms, the four Gospels, and the Acts of the Apostles.

- Point to the pictures, and ask your child what comparison he or she can see between them. (Each shows good news being shared.)

Sharing the Scriptures

- Ask your child if he or she knows what a shepherd does. If not, look for resources on the Internet or at your library that might help illustrate the job of a shepherd.

- Read the story of "One Lost Sheep," and discuss your reactions. You may want to dramatize the story by playing a modified version of hide-and-seek. Take turns playing the roles of the shepherd and lost sheep.

- After reading the story look at the illustration and have your child share what he or she sees happening.

Exploring the Rite

- Clarify for your child the boldfaced words on pages 26 and 27. Be sure he or she fully understands them before you read the text.

- Read together "Words of Love and Mercy" and the *We Ask* question and answer. Discuss any questions your child may still have about the material on these pages.

- *My Reconciliation Book*—Allow your child time to complete pages 3–5 and 12. You might want to play some relaxing music for him or her. You can review the pages with your child now or when you go through the chapter's *Sharing Page*.

Living Reconciliation

- Read the directions for the exercise on page 28. Suggested Scripture passages include:

  "You, Lord, are my shepherd. I will never be in need" *(Psalm 23:1)*.

  "Nothing can separate us from God's love" *(Romans 8:38)*.

  "Always be glad because of the Lord!" *(Philippians 4:4)*.

  "Sing a new song to the Lord!" *(Psalm 96:1)*.

  If you or your child have another favorite Scripture passage, use it for the bookmark.

- Pray together "The Lord Is Good" on page 29. Begin and end with the Sign of the Cross. You might choose to read the body of the prayer to your child, while inviting him or her to join with you for the refrain.

More to Share

- Create with your child a family newspaper. Ask him or her to interview as many family members as possible to find out what good news they have received lately. Help type the stories into a newspaper or newsletter format. You can model it after your local newspaper, adding your own name to the heading. Send copies of the finished newsletter to other family members and friends who might enjoy sharing in the news.

- *Sharing Page*—Complete the Chapter 3 *Sharing Page* together.

- Books and Videos—You may wish to share these additional resources, available from the library, your diocesan media center, or publishers' catalogs.

For children and families

Celebrating Reconciliation with Children (6-part video series) (produced by Salt River Production Group; BROWN-ROA).

   Segment 3: We Hear Good News is designed for use with this chapter.

The Lost Sheep, by Debbie Tafton O'Neal (Judson Press).

   A retelling of Jesus' parable about God's mercy.

For adults

How to Read and Pray the Gospel (Liguori).

   A handbook for living God's word every day.

Liturgy: Becoming the Word of God (audio) (Franciscan Communications/St. Anthony Messenger Press).

   Popular lecturer Megan McKenna speaks about living God's word.

Preparing for the Celebration

Read

"The word of God which you receive by your ear, hold fast in your heart. For the word of God is the food of the soul."

—*Saint Gregory the Great*

Reflect

How well do I listen to God's good news in the Scriptures?

How can reflecting on God's word help me avoid sin and seek forgiveness?

Pray

God of kindness and mercy,
you have given me your word as a beacon for
      my journey.
Help me share the light of the gospel
with my child
who is preparing to celebrate your loving
      forgiveness
in the Sacrament of Reconciliation.
Amen.

CHAPTER 4
WE LOOK AT OUR LIVES
Pages 30–37

See *Catechism of the Catholic Church, #1777–1783.*

Background
At various times in our lives we may think of conscience as an external, friendly voice that consistently nudges us in the correct moral direction. The truth, of course, is more wonderfully complex. Conscience may indeed be thought of as a voice, but it is an internal voice, a harmony of intellect and reason, emotion and will knitted into our personhood by God. And in order to rely on the nudgings of that voice, we must take the responsibility of forming our conscience, nurturing it on the law as revealed to us in the Scriptures, in the teachings of the Church, and in the person of Jesus. Fortunately, we have the help of the Holy Spirit. "Our Lord, you bless everyone who lives right and obeys your Law. You bless all those who follow your commands from deep in their hearts" *(Psalm 119:1–2).*

Preparing Your Child at Home

Getting Started
- Read together the Ten Commandments, found on page 57 of your child's book. Ask your child why God gave them to us.
- Pray the opening prayer with your child. Then read the text on pages 30 and 31.
- After you have finished reading, ask your child again why God gave us the commandments. (This time your child should be more aware of the happiness that will result from following the commandments.)

Sharing the Scriptures
- Ask your child to put into his or her own words a one-sentence definition of the Ten Commandments.
- Read the story of "The Great Commandment" with your child. When you've finished reading the text, ask your child to point out the illustration for each part of the story and to describe what is going on in each picture.
- Explain to your child that the man in the story was doing what you have just done—he was putting the Ten Commandments into his own words.

Exploring the Rite
- Clarify the boldfaced words within "How Do We Measure Up?" and *We Ask*, especially the word *conscience*. (You may also need to explain the Beatitudes to your child; the Beatitudes can be found on page 56.) When your child feels comfortable with the terms, read pages 34 and 35.
- Together, make a bracelet, pendant, or sticker (or two) with the letters *WWJD* (for *What Would Jesus Do?*) on it. Encourage your child to use this reminder to evaluate his or her moral choices.
- *My Reconciliation Book*—Allow your child time to complete pages 4 and 10–11. You might want to play some relaxing music for him or her. You can review the pages with your child now or when you go through the chapter's *Sharing Page.*

Living Reconciliation
- Help your child complete the exercise on page 36. Read the directions aloud, and remind your child about his or her responses to your discussions about the commandments and about conscience. Draw the tablets on another sheet of paper, and complete each statement in your own words. When you both have finished, compare your results.
- Pray together the prayer on page 37. Begin and end by making the Sign of the Cross. You might want to read the main text of the prayer and have your child join with you for the refrain.

More to Share

- With your child, draw up Ten Family Commandments. Yours don't necessarily have to parallel the Ten Commandments, but they should express the values your family considers most important for your household. When you have finished, decide on your family's Great Commandment. Present the list to your family, and post it in an important place.
- *Sharing Page*—Complete the Chapter 4 *Sharing Page* together.
- Books and Videos—You may wish to share these additional resources, available from the library, your diocesan media center, or publishers' catalogs.

For children and families

Celebrating Reconciliation with Children (6-part video series) (produced by Salt River Production Group; BROWN-ROA).

   Segment 4: We Look at Our Lives is designed for use with this chapter.

Kevin's Temptation (video) (produced by Twenty-Third Publications; BROWN-ROA).

   A story about making the right choice.

We Ask Forgiveness: A Young Child's Book for Reconciliation (St. Anthony Messenger Press).

   Includes material on examining one's conscience.

For adults

"Examining Your Conscience Today," by George Alliger and Jack Wintz OFM (*Catholic Update*; St. Anthony Messenger Press).

Seven Principles for Teaching Christian Morality (audio) (Franciscan Communications/St. Anthony Messenger Press).

   Tips for parents on communicating Christian values.

Preparing for the Celebration

Read

"What we call conscience is the voice of Divine Love in the deep of our being, desiring union with our will."

—*J. P. Greaves*

Reflect

What image do I have of my conscience?

How do I nourish and form my conscience?

Pray

God of Wisdom,
open my mind and heart to your will,
and shape my conscience with your love.
Send your Spirit to guide my child
to grow in understanding.
Help us make the good and loving choices
you call us to make.
Amen.

CHAPTER 5
WE ASK FORGIVENESS
Pages 38–45

See *Catechism of the Catholic Church,* #1455–1456, 1467.

Background The therapeutic benefits of private confession were recognized by the founders of modern psychoanalysis, who based the analytic process on this ancient ritual. "Confession is good for the soul," the proverb says, and the benefits are far greater than the mere relief we feel when we let go of a painful secret. In the Church's history, private confession grew out of the Celtic monks' practice of sharing one's spiritual progress (or lack of it) with an *anam-cara,* a "soul friend," or spiritual director. Even though we celebrate the Sacrament of Reconciliation in a communal way today, the confession of sin, acceptance of a penance, and absolution are still celebrated privately, except in cases of emergency. This underlines the importance of personal accountability for sin and its consequences and allows the confessor to tailor the penance to be most helpful to the penitent's circumstances. "If you have sinned, you should tell each other what you have done. Then you can pray for one another and be healed" *(James 5:16).*

Preparing Your Child at Home

Getting Started

- Look with your child at the photo on page 38. Ask your child to make up a story about what is happening in the pictures. Talk about times when your child might have been in a similar situation with a sibling or a friend. Did apologizing and making up for the hurt make your child feel better?
- Pray the opening prayer together, and read the text on pages 38 and 39. Clarify with your child the boldfaced words before you begin.
- Ask your child to explain to you the difference between making a mistake and committing a sin. If necessary, read the last paragraph on page 38 again.

Sharing the Scriptures

- Read with your child the story of "The Man Who Changed His Life," and look at the illustration of Zacchaeus perched in the tree.
- Talk about the sins Zacchaeus committed. Then explain to your child that Jesus forgave Zacchaeus because he admitted his wrongdoing, was truly sorry, and promised to make up for cheating people as a sign that he was going to change his life. Explain that we can do the same; no matter what we do, God offers us forgiveness. We have to be sorry and accept it.

Exploring the Rite

- Clarify the boldfaced words on page 43. When your child feels comfortable with the words, read together "Confession and Penance" and the *We Ask* question and answer.
- Talk with your child, in general terms, about what he or she might expect from the experience of confession. Explain the ways in which the sacrament is celebrated in your parish.
- *My Reconciliation Book*—Allow your child time to complete pages 6–7 and 13. You might want to play some relaxing music for him or her. You can review the pages with your child now or when you go through the chapter's *Sharing Page.*

Living Reconciliation

- Help your child complete the exercise on page 44. Read the directions aloud, and remind your child about his or her responses to your discussions about confession and penance and about the Scripture story. Draw a broken vase on another sheet of paper, and draw or write your own responses. When you have both finished, discuss your results.
- Pray together the prayer on page 45. Begin and end by making the Sign of the Cross. You might want to read the main text of the prayer and have your child join with you for the response.

More to Share

- Take time to visit your church's Reconciliation room or confessional. Show your child the components of the space (the screen, the benches or chairs, the Bible). Answer any questions your child may have. The point is to demystify the whole experience for him or her.

- *Sharing Page*—Complete the Chapter 5 *Sharing Page* together.

- Books and Videos—You may wish to share these additional resources, available from the library, your diocesan media center, or publishers' catalogs.

For children and families

Celebrating Reconciliation with Children (6-part video series) (produced by Salt River Production Group; BROWN-ROA).

    Segment 5: We Ask Forgiveness is designed for use with this chapter.

Jesus and the Grumpy Little Man, by Carol Greene (Concordia Press).

The Story of Zacchaeus, by Marty Rhodes Figley (B. Eerdmans).

    Two retellings of the story of Zacchaeus for children.

For adults

"How to Go to Confession," by Leonard Foley OFM (*Catholic Update*; St. Anthony Messenger Press).

The God Who Reconciles (video) (Franciscan Communications/St. Anthony Messenger Press).

    This video uses story, witness, teaching, and song to explore the meaning of the Sacrament of Reconciliation.

Why Go to Confession? Questions and Answers About Sacramental Reconciliation, by Rev. Joseph M. Champlin (St. Anthony Messenger Press).

    A guide to the Rite of Penance.

Preparing for the Celebration

Read

"The confession of evil works is the first beginning of good works."

    —*Saint Augustine*

Reflect

When have I experienced the benefits of confession?

How can I use confession and the receiving of a penance to help my growth in faith?

Pray

Jesus, soul-friend,
help me and my child see you
in the priest who hears our confessions.
May we be open to your loving direction
in the penances we receive.
Give us the courage
to accept responsibility for our wrong choices
and the grace to make better ones.
Amen.

CHAPTER 6
WE GO FORTH IN PARDON AND PEACE
Pages 46–53

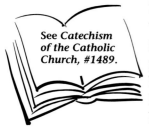

See *Catechism of the Catholic Church, #1489.*

Background

The Sacrament of Reconciliation has the powerful effect of bringing back together that which has been separated or broken—the bond of graced relationship between each person and God, the human community, and all creation. The reference to creation may give us pause. We know that sin disrupts our relationship with God and with others. But why does the Church expressly teach that sacramental absolution reconciles us with creation? The disorder, the radical fracture that sin brings about in our lives, extends to all things because all things came from God's hand and share the same destiny. All creation is called to be returned, in grace, to the wholeness and beauty original sin disrupted. The final return will signal the coming of God's kingdom in fullness. Each time we participate in the Sacrament of Reconciliation, we experience a foretaste of the joy for which we, and all things, were created. "In fact, all creation is eagerly waiting for God to show who his children are. Meanwhile, creation is confused, but not because it wants to be confused. God made it this way in the hope that creation would be set free from decay and would share in the glorious freedom of his children" *(Romans 8:19–21).*

Preparing Your Child at Home

Getting Started

- Clarify the boldfaced words on page 47. When your child feels comfortable with them, pray the opening prayer and read the text. Discuss the pictures and how they relate to the text.

- You will find an Act of Contrition on page 55 of your child's textbook. Read it together, and discuss some of the ideas that are most important to each of you.

Sharing the Scriptures

- Read with your child the story of "The Forgiven Woman."

- Talk with your child about how sorry this woman was. Explain that to be forgiven, we must be truly sorry for the hurt we have caused. Point out the line in the Act of Contrition that states "I am truly sorry for my sins with all my heart."

- Discuss why the people in the illustration reacted the way they did.

Exploring the Rite

- Clarify the boldfaced words on pages 50 and 51. When your child feels comfortable with the terms, read "Contrition and Absolution" and the *We Ask* question and answer.

- Give your child the opportunity to read the Act of Contrition aloud. Explain that he or she needs to be familiar with this or another form of the prayer by the time of First Reconciliation. The Jesus Prayer, found on page 55, may also be used as a simple Act of Contrition.

- *My Reconciliation Book*—Allow your child time to complete pages 8–9 and 14–16. You might want to play some relaxing music for him or her. You can review the pages with your child now or when you go through the chapter's *Sharing Page.*

Living Reconciliation

- Help your child complete the exercise on page 52. Read the directions aloud, and remind your child about his or her responses to your discussions about confession and absolution and about the Scripture story. As your child writes, compose your own Act of Contrition. When you both have finished, compare your results.

- Pray together the prayer on page 53. Begin and end by making the Sign of the Cross. You might want to read the main text of the prayer and have your child join with you for the response.

More to Share

- Create a journal with your child that will include daily entries of how he or she has shared God's love. The entries can note either ways in which your child has learned from a previous wrong choice and made a more loving choice the second time or how he or she has made up for causing hurt. The journal should be bright and colorful and the entries focused on the positive actions of reconciliation.
- *Sharing Page*—Complete the Chapter 6 *Sharing Page* together.
- Books and Videos—You may wish to share these additional resources, available from the library, your diocesan media center, or publishers' catalogs.

For children and families

Celebrating Reconciliation with Children (6-part video series) (produced by Salt River Production Group; BROWN-ROA).

   Segment 6: We Go Forth in Pardon and Peace is designed for use with this chapter.

Jesus Forgives My Sins, by Mary Terese Donze ASC (Liguori).

   A child's book about sacramental absolution.

Skateboard (video) (Franciscan Communications/St. Anthony Messenger Press).

   A parable of Reconciliation in the family.

For adults

Celebrating Reconciliation with Families (2-part video series) (produced by Salt River Production Group; BROWN-ROA).

   Father Joe Kempf helps parents reflect on the meaning of the sacrament.

The Forgiving Family: First Steps Toward Reconciliation, by Carol Luebering (St. Anthony Messenger Press).

   Living the grace of Reconciliation at home.

Preparing for the Celebration

Read

"Being holy doesn't mean never falling into sin. It means being able to say, 'Yes, Lord, I have fallen a thousand times. But thanks to you I have got up again a thousand and one times.'"

—*Dom Helder Camara*

Reflect

What are the most important effects of Reconciliation for me?

How does the possibility of God's forgiveness influence my own growth in holiness?

Pray

Dear God
—forgiving Father, redeeming Son, sanctifying Spirit—
thank you for the Sacrament of Reconciliation and your call to holiness.
Help me guide my child to trust in your mercy and turn to you with confidence
while growing in faith and love.
Amen.

elebrating Other Sacraments

This section of the Teaching Guide offers background, suggestions, and resources about preparing children for sacraments other than First Reconciliation.

First Communion

Church norms dictate that children of catechetical age (usually second grade) be prepared for First Reconciliation before First Communion. Ideally, preparation for these two sacraments should not be combined, and celebration of First Reconciliation should precede celebration of First Communion.

If you or the children's families are preparing children to celebrate First Communion, you will find BROWN-ROA's *Celebrating Our Faith: Eucharist* a complete resource.

Confirmation and First Eucharist

Many Catholic communities today are working toward restoring the original order of the Sacraments of Initiation by inviting baptized children to celebrate Confirmation before or at the same time as First Communion. Pages S2–S4 of this section offer more background on this practice for your information.

If you or the children's families are preparing children to celebrate Confirmation at the time of First Communion, you will find supplemental lesson plans in the Teaching Guide accompanying BROWN-ROA's *Celebrating Our Faith: Eucharist*.

Because children should be in a state of grace to be confirmed and to receive First Communion, they should ordinarily be prepared to celebrate First Reconciliation before Confirmation and First Communion. Diocesan and pastoral guidelines will shape this sequence, but a general practice would be to celebrate First Reconciliation with a communal service, followed some weeks later by the celebration of Confirmation and First Communion. The Rite of Confirmation indicates that Confirmation of children of catechetical age should be celebrated separately from First Communion and outside a Mass, but you should follow the direction of your diocese.

The Sacraments of Initiation

On occasion children are presented by their families for First Reconciliation/First Communion preparation without the children's having been baptized. In these cases, families should be directed to enroll their children in a children's catechumenate program, where the children will be prepared to celebrate all three Sacraments of Initiation— Baptism, Confirmation, and First Communion— at the same time (generally at the Easter Vigil, with adult catechumens). One available resource is BROWN-ROA's *Children's Catechumenate* program. If there is no children's catechumenate available to families in your area, the pastoral team should work with families and children to prepare them for all three Sacraments of Initiation.

In the case of children preparing for initiation, First Reconciliation does *not* precede First Communion. Baptism frees the child from original sin and all personal sin, and Confirmation and First Communion are celebrated at the same ceremony. Children who have celebrated all three Sacraments of Initiation may be prepared subsequently for the Sacrament of Reconciliation and may celebrate this sacrament for the first time at a later parish celebration or individually.

The Order of Initiation

Most twentieth-century Western-Rite Catholics, baptized as infants, celebrated First Communion at the "age of discretion" (sometime around the age of seven) and were confirmed some years later. Not until the revival of the Rite of Christian Initiation of Adults (RCIA), with its profound effects on the way Catholics look at the process of initiation, did most of us ever question the order in which we celebrated the sacraments. Few of us understood that rather than "the way it's always been," the Baptism-First Communion-Confirmation sequence has been the norm for only about a hundred years.

In the early centuries of the Church, initiation (which was most commonly the conversion of adults to Christianity) was understood as a process. The three sacraments —Baptism, Confirmation, and Eucharist—which we now see as separate, were experienced as one continuous movement. The new Christian was bathed in the waters of Baptism, anointed in Confirmation, and invited to the table of the Eucharist in one integral ceremony. This unity is still preserved in Eastern Rite Churches.

The minister of initiation was the bishop, the successor of the apostles and the shepherd of the local Christian community. But as the number of Christians grew, it became more difficult for the bishop to be present to initiate all those wishing to join the faith community. Confirmation and reception of First Communion were deferred until the bishop could get to the widespread parishes. (We still see this today in the practice of celebrating Confirmation once a year at the bishop's annual parish visit.) And as infant Baptism became the more common practice, Confirmation and First Communion were looked on as sacraments of maturity. Full initiation into the Church became a process lasting more than twelve years.

Until the beginning of the twentieth century, however, the original order of the Sacraments of Initiation was still preserved. Children baptized as infants were usually confirmed and invited to the Eucharistic table around the age of twelve or thirteen. It was Pope Pius X, in 1910, who responded to a decline in the number of Catholics receiving Communion regularly by moving the age of First Communion (and First Reconciliation) to the "age of discretion." That decree opened the Eucharist to children, but—with some exceptions, such as the practice in many Latin American Catholic communities—left Confirmation isolated and destroyed the order of initiation.

The theology that sees Confirmation as an adolescent or young-adult rite of passage grew out of this change. In reviving the RCIA and renewing the Rite of Confirmation, the Church left to the discretion of local bishops the minimum age for Confirmation, which led to the situation at the end of the twentieth century, which allowed Confirmation to be celebrated at every possible age from infancy to adulthood.

reparation for Confirmation

What are the practical considerations involved in preparing young children to celebrate Confirmation? How can this preparation be coordinated with preparation for First Reconciliation and First Communion?

It's important to distinguish between the situations of baptized and unbaptized children. Children who have not yet been baptized should be prepared for all three Sacraments of Initiation as part of the parish's catechumenate. These children should have their own catechists and should meet separately from adult catechumens, but they should follow the same schedule and should ideally be initiated with adult catechumens at the Easter Vigil celebration.

With children who have been baptized and whose families present them for First Communion and First Reconciliation preparation, catechesis for Confirmation is actually fairly simple. Remember that Confirmation is not a sacrament of maturity, nor is preparation for Confirmation a kind of "final exam" in the faith. Christian service projects, a familiar and beneficial component of many adolescent Confirmation programs, are not a requirement of catechesis for Confirmation. The *Catechism of the Catholic Church* reminds us that the necessary catechesis for Confirmation, especially when it is seen properly as a Sacrament of Initiation, consists in helping the candidate draw closer to Jesus Christ, become more familiar with the working of the Holy Spirit, and remain open to his or her call to live the baptismal commitment.

BROWN-ROA's *Celebrating Our Faith: Eucharist* Teaching Guide contains eight reproducible lessons for Confirmation preparation, correlated to the eight chapters of the First Communion book.

arish and Family Involvement

The decision to prepare children for Confirmation at the time of First Reconciliation and First Communion should be undertaken by the whole parish community after consultation with diocesan leadership. Because this process varies from the practice familiar to many parishioners—including the children's families—care should be taken to provide sufficient education and discussion in advance of enrollment. This can be accomplished through parish bulletin inserts, family meetings, and adult education forums.

At the very least, parents and other adult family members should be provided with background on the place of Confirmation in the order of initiation. This background should be given during a sacramental preparation meeting. The material in this introductory section may be adapted for use with families. You may also wish to have a member of the diocesan or parish catechetical team provide background for families.

While the bishop remains the ordinary minister of Confirmation, in most cases children being confirmed at the time of First Eucharist will be confirmed by the pastor or another priest who has been involved in their catechetical journey—if possible, the same priest who will preside at their First Communion Mass. This priest should also be invited to speak with the children, their families, and their sponsors about the sacrament.

Sponsors

The role of the sponsor in the Sacraments of Initiation is to stand for the support of the Christian community throughout the initiate's journey of faith. In the case of infants and young children, the sponsors are usually referred to as godparents because they have the additional responsibility of supporting the child's family in the task of raising children in the faith.

The Church highly recommends that godparents continue the commitment they made at Baptism by acting as the child's Confirmation sponsors. This highlights the connection between the sacraments. However, for various reasons it may not always be possible for godparents to act as sponsors. Baptized children being confirmed before First Communion may, with the help of their families, choose a Confirmation sponsor of either sex, even a parent, to stand with them at the ceremony. The canonical requirements for sponsors are that they are spiritually qualified for the office and that they meet the following criteria:

- They must be sufficiently mature. (In most dioceses a minimum age of 16 is the norm.)
- They must belong to the Catholic Church and have been fully initiated (have celebrated Baptism, Confirmation, and the Eucharist).
- They must not be prohibited from exercising this office by any other law. In the case of children preparing for First Communion, parish prayer partners may be considered excellent choices for Confirmation sponsors if godparents or other suitable sponsors are not available.

 # Resources

The following books, videos, and *Catholic Update* articles, available from your diocesan resource library or from publishers' catalogs, offer further background on the Sacraments of Initiation and the celebration of these sacraments with young children.

Anointing with the Spirit: The Rite of Confirmation/The Use of Oil and Chrism, by Gerard Austin OP (The Liturgical Press).

A Child's Journey: The Christian Initiation of Children, by Rita Burns Senseman (St. Anthony Messenger Press).

The Christian Initiation of Children: Hope for the Future, by Robert D. Duggan and Maureen Kelly (Paulist Press).

The Church Speaks About Sacraments with Children: Baptism, Confirmation, Eucharist, Penance (Liturgy Training Puiblications).

"Confirmation: A Deepening of Our Christian Identity," by Carol Luebering (*Catholic Update*; St. Anthony Messenger Press).

"Confirmation: Anointed for Fuller Witness," by Sandra de Gidio OSM (*Catholic Update*; St. Anthony Messenger Press).

Doors to the Sacred, by Joseph Martos (Triumph Books/Liguori).

The Eucharist as Sacrament of Initiation, by Nathan Mitchell (Liturgy Training Publications).

God Speaks to Us in Feeding Stories, by Mary Ann Getty-Sullivan (Liturgical Press).

God Speaks to Us in Water Stories, by Mary Ann Getty-Sullivan (Liturgical Press).

"First Communion: Joining the Family Table," by Carol Luebering (*Catholic Update*; St. Anthony Messenger Press).

Focus on the Sacraments (video) (BROWN-ROA).

"Have Sacraments Changed?" by Mark R. Francis CSV (*Catholic Update*; St. Anthony Messenger Press).

Lord of Light: Confirmation (video) (BROWN-ROA).

Preparing Children for Liturgy: A Catechist's Guide, by Armandine Kelly (Resource Publications).

Rethinking the Sacraments: Holy Moments in Daily Living, by Bill Huebsch (Twenty-Third Publications).

The Sacraments: How Catholics Pray, by Thomas Richstratter OFM (St. Anthony Messenger Press).

Understanding the Sacraments (video) (St. Anthony Messenger Press/Franciscan Communications).

Words Around the Font, by Gail Ramshaw (Liturgy Training Publications).

Words Around the Table, by Gail Ramshaw (Liturgy Training Publications).

Your Child's First Communion: A Look at Your Dreams—Reflections for Parents on the Meaning of the Eucharist, by Carol Luebering (St. Anthony Messenger Press).